Legacy

by Leslie Schonfeld
with Emily Gehman

Kathie
May God Bless
you as you learn
to live your legacy

Love ~
Leslie
John 1:18

Legacy

Leslie Schonfeld

With Emily Gehman

Dragonfly Ministry
2016

Legacy by Leslie Schonfeld with Emily Gehman

ISBN: 978-0-578-17893-6

Copyright ©2016 by Leslie Schonfeld

Requests for information should be directed to
Dragonfly Ministry 2460 Trinity Ct. Oxford, MI 48371

Cover photography by Mary Fix from In His Image Photography

First printing February 2016/Printed in the United States of America

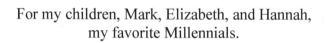
For my children, Mark, Elizabeth, and Hannah,
my favorite Millennials.

Contents

Acknowledgements

I can't go any further without thanking Emily Gehman. A Millennium herself, she did both content and copy editing on this project. Emily is a speaker and author, as well as editor of Shattered.com an online Christian magazine. Make sure you take time to check it out.

To my family. Your ongoing encouragement helped me complete this journey. I love you. Dave, my wonderful husband, thank you for reminding me that this is Kingdom work. To my children, Mark, Elizabeth, and Hannah thanks for making me look good. You inspire me to take risks and dream big!

To the young women who choose to live this adventure with me. Thank you for all you have given me and directing me to my purpose.

An Invitation from Leslie

Me? Mentor? I didn't set out to do this. I fell into it. Delighted by time with my young friends, it became my passion. Each of us influence other people. We don't always recognize this. There is a need for mentors. Mentors leave an impression that lasts a life time. This biblical tradition is essential in nurturing the next generation. One on one ministry is their desire. They need mentoring but more importantly they want mentoring. Join me as we breathe new life into this old tradition. Learn to build your legacy.

Chapter One: Building A Legacy

As a young mom, I was mentored by Elizabeth. A wonderful teacher, she saw in me a glimpse of who I could become. Her original intention was to encourage me to lead and teach within the women's ministry at my church. As our relationship developed, she became my friend, and she even nurtured my desire to write.

I joined the Women's Ministry at my church, in my early thirties. My responsibility was hospitality, specifically overseeing food preparation. Elizabeth invited me to share my cooking talents with a group of ladies. This time however, I was asked to teach how to cook the dessert before it was served. What I didn't realize was Elizabeth had been observing me. She recognized a teaching talent in me that was not yet utilized, and cooking dessert was only the beginning.

I always knew I wanted to teach God's word, but I didn't know how to initiate that process. I prayed for opportunity. I was determined to allow the Holy Spirit to lead, but I was afraid any movement I made would be outside of God's will. I will never forget the phone call that came on a bright June morning. Elizabeth was looking for women to mentor into Bible Study leadership. She was wondering if I would be interesting in joining two other women in a year long process. After that year, the three of us would share the Bible Study leadership at our church. I didn't hesitate to say yes—this is what I had waited for! As the year progressed, so did our friendship. Soon we were discussing more than Bible Study—we were sharing our lives.

Elizabeth possesses a plethora of knowledge about Christian and Hebrew ancestry. (See Romans 11:11-31.) She shared this knowledge in Bible studies and in her home. She even invited my family to partake in Passover meals. She poured into me a wealth of information that helped me understand my identity in Christ.

But it wasn't just knowledge she poured into me. Elizabeth knew me, and saw what I was good and what I was not-so-good at. She saw things I didn't see; she exposed flaws and encouraged gifts. Not only did she teach, but she listened. Introverted, she chose her words thoughtfully. I was the extrovert to her introvert, and often had ten times as many words as she did! But she listened closely to every one of them. She was a wonderful sounding board and I have learned much not only from her knowledge but also her technique.

> The potential is in you because you have Jesus in you. He is greater than your past.

"You realize I didn't give you any advice," Elizabeth would say with a chuckle. "I just had to wait until you heard what was in your head. You came to the conclusion without me."

That may be true, but I needed help untangling that mess. I'm a verbal processor; I needed someone who loved me enough to patiently listen to all the details, all the bunny trails, and finally determine the conclusion. This is one of the tools I bring to the young women I know. I love them because I was loved. I pass on the legacy I was given.

Be An Elizabeth

Maybe you didn't have an Elizabeth in your life—don't let that stop you from being an Elizabeth for someone else! The potential is in you because you have Jesus in you. He is greater than your past. Put Him in the center of your relationships and watch Him work. You can do this. Be the woman you wished you had in your life.

The Millennial generation—which includes those born between 1980 and 1997— is a unique group. As with any new generation, society has nurtured them to be different than the generations that came before them. They are inclusive, yet they don't easily trust. They are passionate but are easily discouraged. They are responsible but don't always follow through. They are big dreamers but are frustrated by hard work. They need direction but don't always want to hear what you have to say. But more than anything, this generation wants to be heard. Not to tell you what to do but so that they can work through their struggles and become the people God has designed.

Are you willing to listen?

I know, I know—I can hear your protest now: "But I don't have anything to offer!"

That's not true. Discipleship is not about your accomplishments. You don't need an impressive resume or a string of letters behind your name to be a mentor. Discipleship is about sharing your struggles as well as your victories. Sharing life is more important than sharing advice. Availability plays a

> Sharing life is more important than sharing advice.

stronger role than teaching knowledge. You have wisdom to share but your confidence comes from your identity in Christ, not your achievements. You are fully equipped, and sharing time tells others they they are important. Sharing life—like Jesus did with His disciples— just takes availability. Will you make yourself available?

It really is that easy. Of course, you'll need some basic tools: prayer, a willing heart, a voice to say hello, time, and the ability to get out of your comfort zone. But that's what this book is for. In the coming pages, we'll burst these ideas wide open, helping you become confident in developing caring relationships with younger women. You'll learn why the rising generation needs you, and you'll gain tools to empower you. And of course, I'll share some personal stories to give you more understanding of the Millennial generation beyond the stereotypes and generalizations.

Are you ready to build a legacy? Let's go

Chapter Two—Who Am I?

I grew up in a Christian home and went to church every Sunday. I always felt loved in my family, and words of encouragement were spoken over me regularly. My parents told me Jesus loved me as I was. I trusted my parents, but when I went about my daily life I heard a different story. Other kids told me I wasn't pretty, my glasses were too thick, my hair too stringy, and I didn't have stylish clothes. In the world's eyes I was a nerdy, homely mess—and I believed them.

I never talked about it to anyone because I didn't think there was anything I could do about it. It was what it was.

But when I went away to college, life became a bit more complicated. My roommate was a self-proclaimed atheist, and boy, did she challenge my faith. The problem was I could not tell her why I believed Jesus was God; I had just accepted it as truth but never investigated it for myself. As I began to question, I prayed a great deal and God began to reveal Himself in a personal way. As I joined Bible studies, asked questions, and pursued God, He became very real to me. As I got to know Him and learned who He really was, He taught me who I really was. The more I understood how I fit into His Kingdom the more confident I became.

As my confidence grew, I realized something else was happening: I became more attractive to other people. I love people and am an incredibly relational being, but my natural personality was hidden because of the victimization I experienced as a kid. When that pain was healed, my true identity was revealed—I am His child, and no one can take that from me.

Who Am I?

This is a question we each face. Labels are everywhere in our society. We categorize ourselves. I'm a mom, wife, leader, teacher, follower, but these titles don't drive me. The question for each of us—for you—is what is at the core of your identity?

But what if instead of searching among the label options our culture presents, you searched in the Word of God for how He labels you? What does God call you?

First of all, Jesus' sacrifice—the Gospel—gives you the label of a Child of God. "So you have not received a spirit that makes you fearful slaves. Instead, you received God's Spirit when he adopted you as his own children. Now we call him, "Abba, Father" (Romans 8:15 NLT).

> Your identity and your confidence come from your relationship with Jesus.

This is the source of your confidence. I know I am accepted because of Jesus—He endured rejection in order to bring me acceptance. I know I am worthy because He created me and He loves me. I follow Him as He leads the way in advancing His Kingdom. All of these things I must remind myself of daily. Otherwise I'll lose track of why I do what I do—and I imagine you might, too.

I had to get to know Jesus in a relationship with him in order to truly know who I am. And I had—and still have to—remember what I do does not define who I am.

Let me say that again. What you do does not define who you are.

If you have a relationship with Jesus, you are a Child of God—and it's a permanent adoption! As His child, you serve Him out of love, not in search of acceptance. Your adoption as His child implies acceptance into His family, no matter what. You are a child of God. Nothing you can do can change that fact, and you can never be disowned or refused the rights of this divine adoption.

Yes, you have rights.

John 1:12 states we have been given the right to God's family when we believe on him. It says "But to all who believed him and accepted him, he gave the right to become children of God (John 1:12 NLT, emphasis mine). When you believe, God accepts and adopts you as a family member; your imperfections do not disqualify you, but you trade your debt of sin for the rights of being God's own family member.

When I read John 1:12, I sense the Holy Spirit penetrating my being, and He whispers, "It is your right to grasp. Share it. Because it is their right, too."

So, I did a bit of study on this word, right, and when I found it in Strong's Concordance[1], I learned it is multi-faceted, with a deeper meaning than I originally thought. It means privilege, force, capacity, competency, freedom, mastery, delegated influence, authority, jurisdiction, power, right, strength. See what I mean? It's a huge word!

Let's look at each of those words associated with right and seek the deep truth behind this word exousia. Read the following paragraph, take time to search the Scriptures, and let each word sink into your spirit. Do you believe these things about yourself? If you have a relationship with Jesus then you have been given—you have the rights—to each one.

He gives us the privilege, the gift of family. We are His children—I Peter 4:16.

We have the force necessary to change our identity, our family name—Colossians 2:9-20.

We are granted the capacity to enter His family. It is done, we are to accept the gift.

This gives us the competency to represent His family—2 Corinthians 5:20.

He empowers us with all we need through His Holy Spirit—2 Peter 1:3.

We are freed from sin to be part of His holy family—Galatians 4:5.

He forgives and forgets and empowers us to resist; temptation is present but He strengthens our resistance and we learn to overcome it. This delivers mastery over sin—Romans 6:6.

We live as eternal beings, residents of His Kingdom. We have His delegated influence and authority over darkness in this world—I Peter 2:9.

The power to speak life is ours, in Jesus' name, thus we have jurisdiction that comes with His Kingdom. We have authority over evil—Ephesians 6:12.

We have the power necessary to remain in His family. Nothing is strong enough to remove us from God's family, except our own free will—John 10:28.

We have the right to be called His child. He has given us His name—Christian. He strengthens us to continue in faith as His child—Philippians 4:13.

Did you get all that?

Now go back and re-read each statement, but this time, say your name with the word "has" in each sentence. For example, for the first one I would say, "Leslie has the privilege, the gift of family. Leslie is His child."

No, seriously…go do it.

The depth here is overwhelming! How do you respond to the magnitude of this gift of adoption and its rights? It is a personal promise; your response is to trust Him no matter the circumstance. He is there; rely on Him when you step out in faith. Live as His child. That is your response.

The Message Bible sums it up beautifully. "Who believe he was who he claimed and would do what he said, He made them to be their true selves, their child-of-God selves" (John 1:12 MSG). All the lies heaped on you through circumstances and hurtful people are washed away. You are not what they said. You are who God says you are, and He has given you that right. Doubt is not welcome in the home of God's child.

Your confidence is rooted in your identity. When you know who you are, you are ready to move on and help others know who they are.

When It's Not Always That Easy

But wait. That's not always the case, is it? There are some days when that confidence sticks and some days it doesn't. Sometimes

insecurity trumps action; we're self-focused instead of God-driven. Doubt triumphs over direction.

I see this happen in our dog, Tessie. She performs amazing tricks—or at least she thinks it's a trick. She really loves people but isn't allowed on the furniture in our home. Wanting attention, she will first put one foot on the couch. Averting her eyes, she thinks she's hiding, so she then places a second foot on the couch. Pausing, she waits for the reprimand. If nothing is said, she attempts to place her third foot on the couch. And finally, balancing all three legs, draws up the fourth leg and looks at you like she has always been there. Her slow-motion antics are entertaining, to say the least.

But isn't that what doubt does? It encroaches the same way. Uninvited, it wiggles its way in, paw by paw, wearing a disguise of truth. Sitting with it, I question myself, especially in regard to mentoring: "Am I doing what the Lord is asking me to do? She is so young; I don't have anything in common with her. She won't want to talk to me. I'll wait until she approaches me." A momentary panic grips my heart, and I can't hear the Lord respond. Doubt gives way to fear as self-focus looms large. I forget that doubt is the opposite of faith; God's voice is lost in the din of insecurity, where failure feeds. It's a cycle not easily broken.

But God is always with you. When you don't hear Him, your attention needs to be refocused, remembering who you are—adopted, accepted, and loved as a family member. Your identity and your confidence come from your relationship with Jesus. Prayer and worship can help move your focus from your insecurities back to that relationship, from your doubts to His glory.

But I know, I know. It's not always easy. Doubt and insecurity were my friends for a long time. Recently I recognized there were still remnants of those old wounds. As I was cleaning out a drawer of old photo albums, a photo fell out. It was an old yellowed Polaroid of me in the seventh grade. I showed it to my son, Mark, because it was proof of my participation on our math team. He saw it and said, "Hey, when was Elizabeth (referring to my daughter) on a math team?" My response? "How could you say that? That's me, not Elizabeth! Elizabeth is so beautiful and I was so ugly!"

Do you hear the lie I had believed for so long? I thought Mark had made a drastic mistake. So I found Elizabeth and showed her the picture. You know what she said? "When was I on a math team?"

It was so revealing to me. Traces of my insecurity were still there in my heart, creeping up at the silliest times. It was a stray thought I hadn't taken captive (2 Corinthians 10:5). I bet you have some of those floating around too.

I continually have to remind myself not to be too busy for my relationship with Jesus. I have to intentionally, regularly, invite Him into my day—but not because of ritual, because of relationship. A ritual would mean ticking off the to-do list so we keep in good standing. It requires only mental assent and simple knowledge of Him. But the relationship is a experiential knowledge of Jesus—not an academic knowledge. It's time spent with Him, meeting Jesus in the Holy place. You are set apart for Him through your relationship with Him (Psalm 4:3).

A Not-So-Shining Example

I love Gideon because I can relate to his story found in Judges 6-8. God told Gideon he was a "valiant warrior." Gideon rung his hands and said, "Are you sure, God? I don't feel like one."

I am both comforted and challenged by this conversation between God and Gideon, because it looks a lot like what happens in my life.

When God approached Gideon He was hiding—Judges 6:11.

When God identified him as a warrior, he questioned God—Judges 6:13.

Gideon said he wasn't gifted—Judges 6:15.

Gideon asked for proof—Judges 6:17.

Gideon was afraid—Judges 6:22.

After a struggle with doubt, he was obedient but in the dark. He stayed hidden—Judges 6:27.

Gideon again questioned God and asked for a sign—Judges 6:38-39.

I love God's patience with Gideon. He continued to instruct and wait for Gideon to get it. Long story short—Gideon became the warrior God declared him to be. He found the courage necessary through his faith. He no longer had to test the instructions he received, he just followed them. God had shown himself faithful to Gideon, and in turn Gideon was faithful to God.

I am comforted God allows us to see this example. It helps me recognize that insecurity is a universal human challenge. I'm not the only one—and neither are you! But it also reminds me we need to overcome it. Gideon learned to trust God, the one who produces victory.

When you lack confidence in yourself, remember it is God who provides your success, not you. Your confidence needs to be rooted in

God's power and God's strength. He will complete His work (Philippians 1:6).

Be courageous, valiant warrior, even when afraid. It's totally okay to seek encouragement as Gideon did. But you must step out and do it! The results are in God's control. Trust Him for His outcome. Push through the obstacles. Most of them are only in your mind anyway. You are God's child, with His acceptance, His rights, destined to do His work. Persevere and do the hard work. God is with you.

Conquering Doubt

Do you, like Gideon, question God's direction? You're not alone. But it's time to break down the wall of doubt.

Spend time with Jesus. Seek Him: "When doubts filled my mind, your comfort gave me renewed hope and cheer" (Psalm 94:19 NLT). Often simply seeking Him for Him soothes more than seeking Him for answers. Press in to enjoy His presence. Here He will reveal your genuine identity. Sing a Psalm to Him. Give Him a list of blessings He has given you. Enjoy Him; He is your beloved. It will realign your spirit and remind you of your true identity.

As you continue this practice, it becomes easier to dismiss doubt. Doubt is the opposite of faith, and if you keep feeding doubt, you are starving faith. But on the other hand, if you feed faith,

> If you feed faith, you'll starve doubt.

you'll starve doubt. Don't chastise yourself for insecurity; that doesn't help. Self-deprecation does not draw you to righteousness; Jesus does. Instead, take action against insecurity. Do not give up. Feed your faith.

Live a God-Centered life: Doubt is conquered by living a God-centered life. Jesus said to love God with all your heart, soul, and mind (Matthew 22:37, NLT). When He is what you are putting your heart, soul, and mind into—when He is at the center, confidence reigns. When you remember your place in God's Kingdom, a humble confidence is birthed, and you are able to reach out to others. The confidence is not birthed in your own abilities, but in Jesus. Your righteousness, your confidence, your identity, is rooted in Him and your faith in Him, not in your accomplishments—or lack thereof.

Live in Freedom: Your adoption brings freedom—freedom from the sin that tied your legs and kept you from advancing. No more is this true. You are released from the bondage of your past and able to move forward. Each time you starve our doubt by feeding faith, its ability to entwine you weakens.

Filter Criticism: Do not be swayed by the opinions of other people. I know, easier said than done. But important: weigh criticism through your Jesus filter. You must remain teachable and able to take constructive insight, but don't let your faults define your worth. Only Jesus defines your worth. He said you are worth His death—sobering, isn't it? And so beautiful. Don't waste His sacrifice on deprecating self-talk. If the criticism or accusation is unfounded, pray for the source before you confront; ask to see them as Jesus does. It's hard to be offended when you see Him in them.

> Don't waste His sacrifice on Deprecating self-talk.

Be the Example: Whether you realize it or not, the next generation watches the way you live your life. They have a keen sense of a person's character. They can jump to conclusions and assume they know you from just one encounter. Consistency in confidence is important. You mentor with the way you live as well as the words you say. Jesus is reflected in what you do. How are you reflecting Him for those coming behind you?

Keep Learning: That's the teacher in me—always seeking knowledge. Keep learning, delight in God's Word and its wisdom (Proverbs 1:4-5). We always have something to learn. Your personal growth is necessary not only for yourself but also for those you mentor. It sets an example for others as you continue pursuing God through Bible study, worship, and intimate prayer. The more we seek Jesus, the more we will live God's way.

Own Your Mistakes: Perfection is not the goal. If God required perfection, nothing would ever happen, because no one is perfect. Everyone makes mistakes, but authenticity is key. Own the mistakes, take responsibility, ask for forgiveness, and move on. Be real. How you handle your mistakes will say more than if you never made any.

I know none of these things are easy. We are continually buffeted by the woes of this world. I am overwhelmed by evil actions of others. I want to hide. I doubt. Then I remember Gideon who fought and won. I remember Jesus who died so I won't.

And when it gets scary, I remember Stephen.

Acts 6-7 tells Stephen's story, and it also describes him as "a man full of God's grace and power." What a lovely combination! But Stephen isn't the only one described as being full of grace and power. In Acts 4:33 it says, "with great power the apostles continued to testify to the resurrection of the Lord Jesus. And God's grace was so powerfully at work in them all" (NIV). The words for grace used here (both pistes and charis) mean faith as well as joy. And all the apostles were filled with grace, faith, and power through Jesus Christ!

All of us have this grace. All of us. Even you! Jesus' completeness has influenced your heart. You have the grace, faith, and power you need for the work ahead.

In Review: You + Jesus = Enough

I spoke to a young friend at a Wednesday night service recently. It was a simple how-are-you exchange and then she asked a question I thought her actions had already answered. "Weren't we going to get together on a regular basis?" I hadn't heard or seen her in a year. I assumed she wasn't interested. But instead of concentrating on who misunderstood, we moved forward. I didn't allow doubt to step in and cause division; we met at the end of that week and will continue to meet monthly.

Discipleship—mentoring—is not about what you have or have not done. Accomplishments may play into it at times but what you share comes from your struggles as well as your victories. Sharing life is more important than sharing advice. Availability is a stronger role than teaching knowledge. Sure, it's always nice to have some wisdom to share but your confidence shouldn't—doesn't—come from your wisdom or achievements or what you do. It comes from your relationship with Jesus.

You may you think you have nothing to offer, but in reality, you already have everything necessary. When you share your time, it shows others they are important. Jesus did this with the disciples—He shared life with them. He told them they were important because of the time He gave them. He was available.

Are you willing to make yourself available?

So, Who Are You?

We started this chapter with a question—who are you?

> Your worth is in one place—Jesus.

If Jesus is your Lord and Savior then you are a child of God. You are my sister in Christ and the daughter of the King. There's your answer. That's where your identity lies and where you confidence comes from—not because of what you do but because of who you are. When doubt creeps in, remind it of your identity and kick it to the curb. Feed for faith and starve your doubt.

Jesus is your foundation. Plant yourself upon Him and rest securely. This is key to mentoring. Your confidence is not determined by acceptance of others, or who they say you are. It is in who God says you are. Your worth is in one place—Jesus. You can take the mentoring risk because of your identity and place in Him.

Risk building a relationship with a few young people. You already have an eternal reward. Share your life with another; it will delight you as God builds your legacy.

Dear Lord, help us know who we are in YOU! You have provided all we need to be confidence to follow your call. Thank you for welcoming us into your family. Empower us to walk daily in this knowledge. In Jesus, AMEN!

Questions:

1. What labels do you wear? Do any overshadow your identity in Christ?

2. Review the translation of exousia Do you struggle in any words described? Write out the scripture associated with that word. Put your name in it, and spend time praying it over your life.

3. What stray thoughts do you battle that attack your confidence? "When doubts filled my mind, your comfort gave me renewed hope and cheer" (Psalm 94:19 NLT). What can you do to put these thoughts to rest?

4. What are you doing to feed your faith and starve your doubt? Do you have an action plan?

Chapter 3 —Get Real

I didn't forget. I misremembered. I was supposed to meet Lauren on a Tuesday but I thought it was Wednesday. So at 8:45 on Tuesday morning my phone reminded me of the appointment. I had 15 minutes to finish what I was doing, shower, dress and get to the coffee shop. And let's be honest—that wasn't happening.

I remembered wrong. Not an excuse but an explanation. It was my fault, so I took ownership of the mistake. Quickly, I texted an apology and requested to reschedule. She understood and we met a few days later instead.

I suppose I could have made up an elaborate story to make myself look better—or at least not as bad. Perhaps a grand excuse that an emergency had arisen and I was the only one to come to the rescue! But what good would that have done? First, I know it wouldn't have worked because I'm a terrible liar. She would have known I wasn't telling the truth. But even worse, my lie would not be an accurate representation of my true confused self. Humbling though it was, I decided it was better to come across as a little daft than untrue.

Authenticity is a characteristic absolutely required by Millennials. They despise figurative masks, and they're really good at sniffing out a fake. They aren't easily fooled; millennials see right through a façade. They prefer raw reality over hidden pretenses. Isn't that true for all of us, though? Probably. But it has jumped to the cultural forefront in recent years. Be yourself and don't play games.

Authenticity does not mean bold or brazen. It is not the same thing as being unique. It means to be true to oneself. It doesn't matter what you look like; you can be main-street-America, dressing the way everyone else does and still be authentic. A genuine person is not concerned with their exterior. A genuine person focuses on reflecting their true character to those around them. Confidence—as we learned in chapter one—does not mean you have it all together; genuine people recognize their imperfection. Confident, authentic people don't let their flaws minimize, or worse yet, paralyze their service to others.

Confidence and authenticity are unique attributes birthed from intimate time with Jesus.

Authenticity is birthed in your relationship with God. The more time you spend with Him, the more time you recognize your true self. It is so closely linked to confidence, I feel I'm repeating myself from the last chapter. But it's still true. Confidence and authenticity are unique attributes birthed from intimate time with Jesus.

Continual refreshment in the presence of the Holy Spirit produces confident and authentic people. The next generation is attracted to these people.

To be sure, authenticity is not easy in our American culture today. Just look at how we greet each other. "How are you?" generates a single reflexive response: "Fine." Somedays we aren't fine, yet we say so anyway. Ironically, a young man from England pointed this out to me.

"You aren't real in America. Out in public everyone is fake. You won't see that in a Brit."

I haven't spent a lot of time in British culture to know how much truth is in his statement. But I do know I hear "fine" a great deal.

So the question is: how does a person become and stay authentic in this character-crippling world? I don't think the answer is to list all our cares to everyone we greet. The grocery clerk doesn't need (or want!) to hear about your cat puking on the carpet. But it's okay to say you've had a rough day. You can be honest and real without complaining about everything. It's not so much what you say, but how you say it. Don't fake it 'til you make it. Be your real self. Take some notes from John the Baptist.

John the Baptist was the epitome of authenticity. Unique and individualistic, he marched to the beat of the Holy Spirit. In Matthew 3, I am struck by the remarkable life of this man. He was not influenced by other's opinions, yet his uniqueness drew others to him. His confidence did not waver.

John was related to Jesus as his cousin. Elizabeth, John's mother, had a close relationship with Mary, Jesus' mother. God told Zechariah, John's father, of John's coming, though Elizabeth was unable to have children. Yet John's life path was described to Zechariah before his birth. God paved the way for John's unique impact on the world. (Read Elizabeth and Zechariah's story in Luke 1.)

John grew up with the knowledge of his prophesied birth and life. So he prepared for his mission by living in the wilderness. He was gifted with the spirit and power of Elijah (Luke 1:17) but he did not try to mimic Elijah. Unabashed by local custom, he survived on honey and locusts. He was viewed as a fanatic by many around him.

But John lived a life that reflected his faith. Don't take this for granted—his faith had to be big. He knew what was said of him—that he would prepare the way for the Messiah—but he had yet to see it happen. We now know how his life played out, but as he was living it, he couldn't see the future. John had promises, predictions, and prophesies, but no outline or step-by-step life plan. This blows my mind. How do you live up to such expectation? Surely only with God can this be possible.

John lived his life to the fullest. Each day his purpose was to prepare his followers' hearts to accept Jesus. Passionately, he preached repentance, uncertain when his mission would be complete. Many found their Messiah in Jesus because John pointed the way. We was even privileged to baptize Jesus. This was culmination of John's ministry.

As Jesus' influence increased, John faded to the background. Was there an inner struggle here as John's fame diminished? Perhaps, but we don't know. His ego had to die; he had to accept this was not about him. Charismatic by nature, he had to give that gift over to God, in a breathtaking act of faith. But he did not escape the human propensity to doubt; we know his faith wavered as he sat in jail, and sent his disciples to ask Jesus if He really was the one John had been preaching about. Jesus pointed to the evidence to assure them He was. (See Matthew 11.) Soon after that John was beheaded.

John's example screams across the millennia to all Christians. It can never be about what you get. It is not to be about your fame. It is not about feeling good about yourself; it's always about following Jesus.

Now think about this. What if John had waited? What if he thought his life's calling wasn't worth the locusts and honey or social rejection? What if he had said "I'm not sure. Let's just see how things work out?" If he had been tentative he may have lived longer, to be sure. Risk involves a price and John paid a high one—the ultimate one. I imagine, however, he lived joyfully to the end with no regrets.

> Following Jesus is not safe. But it is not about your comfort. It's about building the Kingdom.

Following Jesus is not safe. But it is not about your comfort. It's about building the Kingdom. (Matthew 28:19) You've probably heard the popular platitude, "The safest place is in the center of God's will." This is true for the spiritual self, but not necessarily the earthly self. John ended up in prison, on the wrong side of political favor, and eventually on the sharp end of the guillotine. None of that sounds even close to safety to me.

But was it worth it? I think John would say it was.

So what does that have to do with you and me? As far as I know, no angel showed up at my conception to announce my grand impact on humanity. It is pretty clear I am not called to wear camel hair. I could handle eating the honey but locusts are out of the question. But I know God has a plan for me, the real me. And one for you, too. The real you.

Are you tentative? Waiting to see how it will play out? Or are you willing to be real, to be authentic, to ask Jesus if He really is who He says He is? To be honest and struggle on the bad days but on the good days, live life to the fullest? Are you willing to be vulnerable, and to follow Jesus' lead no matter where He leads or how that life might end?

As for me, I'm pursuing a heart like that of the locust eater—living each day to the fullest and authentically. I want God to draw out the best in me, the real me. Grey hair and all.

Going Grey

That's right, I have grey hair. Hairs. Lots of them. And I don't dye it. It's not because I think it's wrong or sinful to dye my hair, but it's a reminder for me. Seems silly, doesn't it? But years ago when I played around with hair color, I realized I was not acting like myself. I was trying to be hip characterization of who God made me to be, and I failed. I know dying your hair is no different than wearing makeup, but for me, it became a stumbling block. So I just don't do it. Thankfully, for me, it's becoming more unique to let grey hairs stay grey, and I've even had young children ask what is in my hair. But truthfully, my natural silver highlights remind me to be myself.

And each day I get up with grey hair, my prayer is for God to remove the imitation—to strip me of my attempts to be someone I'm not, and for the real me to be present.

Of course, I want people to like me. But this cannot influence who I choose to be in public. Others' opinion of good or cool or even real doesn't matter. I have to be me. Even if it is boring. Even if I come across as a prude. Even if they don't like me. Well, to be honest, that does make me a little uncomfortable, but you know what? It's not about me.

The next generation examines our lives. They evaluate our authenticity, and keep mental notes on consistency and if we act the same way in all situations. Oh, and they can smell a fake a mile away. As Christians we are called to live life in an honest reflections of Jesus. Live in truth for all to see. We are to be the same person in public and in private.

This does not give an excuse for rudeness. We should behave in an authentic and respectable manner no matter where we are. Don't use authenticity as an excuse for being a jerk. The real you should point to Jesus. The real you should, eventually, look exactly like Jesus. Scary thought, isn't it? Don't worry—everyone falls short of this goal. But it is the target you are pointing toward. Philippians 1 reminds you of your true home, and how your life should reflect that: "Above all, you must live as citizens of heaven, conducting yourselves in a manner worthy of the Good News about Christ. Then, whether I come and see you again or only hear about you, I will know that you are standing together with one spirit and one purpose, fighting together for the faith, which is the Good News" (Philippians 1:27 NLT).

No Masks Allowed

"I left the church because of the hypocrites" is a popular lament these days. The word hypocrites is rooted in the word that means "actor." Actors are never themselves. They play other people, other characters.

Hypocrisy in the church happens when individuals spout Scripture and its related wisdom without actually living it. When you recite verses about worry but live in fear, or easily see the sin of others while ignoring your own, you are acting. You are a hypocrite.

While it's true that everyone needs work, it's not always easy to see it in yourself. But Jesus wasn't kidding when He said to look for the log in your own eye first. Self-examination can be painful but it is a requirement for growth. Thankfully, the Holy Spirit is gentle as your short-comings are revealed. Be vigilant to know yourself and truly be transformed—every day, in His presence—not to beat yourself up but to become more like Him. What a glorious goal!

> He loves you as you are. He has called you into existence for this time and place.

"Conduct yourself worthy of the gospel" (Ephesians 4:1). That is no small feat, and it's certainly a high call. Jesus paid a high price for that call and so you could have the power to accomplish it. But He knows you are not perfect. Take comfort in that. And in the comforter Himself–the holy Spirit, the Advocate, who Jesus shared to help you along the journey (John 14:26). Yield to the Holy Spirit and His fruits will grow in you: love, joy, peace, patience, kindness, goodness, faithfulness, gentleness, and self-control (Galatians 5:22-23).

You are not alone in this battle. Don't settle for the world's standard you may have already attained; continue to nurture these fruits. Be honest in your struggle to reflect Jesus. This makes you vulnerable, but it also makes you real.

Your authenticity and vulnerability draws people to you. Millennials know who's real and who's not. Are you willing to live your life for real, as you were designed? Accept yourself. This produces confidence; not self-confidence but confidence in Jesus. He loves you as you are. He has called you into existence for this time and place. The ones designated for you to mentor will be drawn to you for you. Trust God in that, and don't be afraid to be yourself.

Authenticity is birthed from honesty. Honesty promotes integrity, integrity drives character, and good character is attractive to others. Scripture supports this ideal (Proverbs 20:6,7). Credible people are trusted people. But people who have learned to play a role other than themselves—to be an actor, to be a hypocrite—will be exposed.

The Generation Gap: Get Real

My generation was taught we could do it all. The Millennial Generation recognizes that it's impossible, and they know to look for cracks in the perfect appearance. They know you're faking it. But—get this—perfection and righteousness are not the same. A righteous person is genuine. They do not glorify their imperfections but acknowledge them. Continue to give over your flaws to Jesus. Time in His presence buffs them away. In Philippians 1, Paul writes, "May you always be filled with the fruit of your salvation—the righteous character produced in your life by Jesus Christ—for this will bring much glory and praise to God" (Philippians 1:11, NLT). This is how John the Baptist lived—true to his design and true to the call of God. And in doing that he influenced thousands. Oh, that the same would be said of me!

Being authentic allows you to be true to not only yourself but also to your Creator. This is attractive. You are not required to be cool, or up on all the current fashion trends, language, and technology—thank goodness, right? You are simply called be true to yourself and to live with integrity. The goal is not perfection but righteousness. God is perfecting you but you are not there yet. Somedays I feel the weight of this more than others, and I'm sure you do, too.

But authenticity is not rooted in your feelings. Emotions are reflective of your circumstances not your character. Authenticity is anchored in your character and your true identity. And remember—your identity does not change because Jesus doesn't change.

> Are you willing to be vulnerable, and to follow Jesus' lead no matter where He leads or how that life might end?

Authenticity is key in mentoring. When you mentor it has to be genuine. It must be for the benefit of the rising generation. Paul explains this in 1 Timothy 1:5 (NLT) "The purpose of my instruction is that all believers would be filled with love that comes from a pure heart, a clear conscience, and genuine faith.

Your desire to mentor must be real. Genuine. As you read through these pages, listen to the Holy Spirit. Of course, I believe everyone should mentor—but then again, I'm the author of a book about mentoring, so I guess that goes without saying. But it's important to me. It is in my God-designed DNA. Don't mentor just because you read a book. Don't mentor because you think it might fulfill a need in you. Do this because you know God wants it for you.

It is okay to be unsure; this is normal when venturing into a new area of service. As you take steps of faith, partner it with prayer. Listen to the Lord. Remind yourself you choose this path to help someone else.

Dear Lord: Show us our true identity. Give us wisdom that reflects our authentic self. Help us to tear off our masks without grumbling and complaining. Thank you Lord you made us as reflections of you. Expose the Holy Spirit in us. In Jesus Name AMEN.

Questions:

1. What does it mean to be authentic? Do you find authenticity easy or hard?

2. Read Philippians 2:14. Write a response to this verse.

3. What is one aspect of John the Baptist's life that speaks to you?

4. What is one characteristic you would like to develop in order to be more authentic?

Chapter Four—What's your mentoring personality?

"Are you offering to mentor me?" she asked.

"Yes," I replied.

"I've looked for 18 months for someone to offer that!"

This bold young woman represents the heart of the younger generation. The need is there and it is clear. They may not seek you out because they don't want to be an inconvenience or they may just not know how to ask. But they want mentoring. They need mentoring, and they know it.

But they may not know all that mentoring entails. The truth is mentoring is more than just mentoring. It's not a programmed process. It is living life together. We laugh together, cry together, and share the mundane with each other. Keyword: Together. A mentor is a stable influence whose sole purpose is to communicate that they matter—to the mentor and to God. Mentoring is important because they are not just the future of the church, they are the current church.

The mentoring journey looks different for everyone. Consider this book as a guideline–it's just my story with some tips and tricks of the trade. But you do what works for you. Build relationships that fit you. But the first you think you must do is seek out the younger generation. Initiate a friendship because they are important. Like Paul, we are to look for and raise true children in the faith. (See 1 Timothy 1:2.) Your young friends should not have to look outside your church walls for spiritual parents. Prepare, search, and invite with Jesus as your motivation, and building the kingdom of God as your goal.

> Mentoring is important because they are not just the future of the church, they are the current church.

Yes, it's a huge responsibility, but it is anchored in Jesus, and with Him all things are possible. He is your power and motivation. Love because He loves. He invests in and builds the lives of others through you. You must be both a good teacher AND a good student. As a disciple, you are a follower, or a student of Jesus, and good students follow the example of good teachers. Are you a good student of Jesus? Because you have good students who are following you, whether you know it or not. You are a teacher and a student.

Reach back and remember what it was like to be a student in school. Maybe you were one of the students who easily sought out the teacher for help or affirmation. But chances are, you weren't. The majority of students are not inclined to seek the teacher for anything, but would rather fly under the radar, to keep from embarrassment or rejection. It's no different in today's generation, and it's no different in mentoring.

I know this can be intimidating. Daunting thoughts run through your brain: "I don't know anyone that age. Why would they listen to me? I'm not equipped!" I've felt that way many times. One particular moment comes to mind when I took my daughter to experience her first horseback riding lesson.

My daughter loves horses, and she begged for horseback riding lessons. We found a course through our local community education program, but I did not realize my participation was required. The first step in the class was grooming the horse, starting with cleaning the horse's hooves. She was given instruction and then expected to just step in and do it. She stood there, lost.

"Do you understand what to do?" I asked.

With big eyes she looked at me and shook her head no.

"Okay, this is how you do it." I stepped up to the horse and began to pick her hooves.

Truth be told, I was as unexperienced as my daughter. Never in my life had I been this close to such a large animal. My mind scrambled prayers and grooming steps together. It was a good thing I was listening during the instructions. My daughter watched me and mimicked my actions, and soon, she mastered all she needed to know.

I wanted my daughter to be confident and enjoy this class, though, admittedly, I was scared of the new situation. But I had to take the risk despite my fear because my desire to see her succeed was greater than my fear.

> Your desire to impact a life must exceed the intimidation you feel.

The same is true with mentoring. Your desire to impact a life must exceed the intimidation you feel. And don't worry—the more you do it, the more you practice, the more experienced you become, and though you may still feel intimidated at times, your fear diminishes.

And don't forget, different personalities handle situations in unique ways. Along with experience, you need to understand yourself.

Know Thyself

We already talked about recognizing your identity in Christ and the importance of authenticity in the last chapter. These are characteristics we all share. But you must also embrace what makes you a unique individual. You are a combination of personal and spiritual gifts. Take some time to investigate this part of yourself.

Myers-Briggs Type Indicator (MBTI®) have helped me to understand myself and my personality. I am ENFP: Extroverted, Intuitive, Feeler, and Perceiver. This makes me a natural diplomat. However, organization and completing tasks are difficult for me. I am learning to overcome this inadequacy. I use my phone calendar all the time. I don't want to miss appointments or double book myself—which, as you already know, has happened and will probably happen again. But now that I know this about myself, I have attained the tools to improve on this.

My Spiritual gifts—the ways I can best contribute to the Body of Christ and in a local church— are teaching, exhortation, and wisdom. With this knowledge, I see the possible ways I react to situations. I also understand not everyone will behave in the same manner.

The more we understand ourselves the better we can minister to others. You can find personality tests and spiritual gifts tests online.

Personality theory is not the be-all-end-all of knowing yourself, and while it is important for understanding yourself, you shouldn't find your identity in it. Remember—your identity is in Christ. Don't feel like you have to be pigeonholed by any one personality. Everyone is a blend of the personality types, but most people are strong in one personality or the other. Maybe two. But, regardless of personality, all people were designed for relationship.

Mentoring In The Bible

Before you initiate these relationships, it helps to understand yourself, because your personality effects who you attract. Understanding your strengths and weaknesses will help you better care for everyone in your life.

We can learn from the strengths and weaknesses of the many mentoring pairs in the Bible. As you read about them in the rest of this chapter, you may see a little of yourself in each description. Find yourself in these examples—Moses and Joshua, Ruth and Naomi, Esther and Mordecai, Elijah and Elisha, Mary and Elizabeth, and Paul and Timothy—and learn from their examples so you can better serve the Kingdom of God.

Notice that each pair made a commitment to each other. The older guided the younger. They shepherded them into God's path. Some were short-term relationships and some lasted for years. First, Moses and Joshua.

Moses and Joshua

Moses represents the leadership mentor. Appointed by God to deliver the Hebrew people from Egyptian captivity, Moses recognized he was leading a reclaimed nation. Joshua was appointed to be his assistant—Moses mentored Joshua with a view to Joshua succeeding him. Among many other things, Moses taught Joshua the importance of intimacy with the Lord. Moses talked with God, and he was the only man that we know of, who actually saw God (Exodus 33:17). He patterned intimacy with God in his lifestyle and he invited Joshua to enter God's holy presence as well.

Take a look at Exodus 33:11. "Inside the Tent of Meeting, the Lord would speak to Moses face to face, as one speaks to a friend.

> You pattern for your mentee what a relationship with God looks like.

Afterward Moses would return to the camp, but the young man who assisted him, Joshua son of Nun, would remain behind in the Tent of Meeting" (Exodus 33:11 NLT).

Joshua didn't stay with Moses. He stayed with the Lord.

Catch this now: The relationship between the mentor and the mentee is secondary. Your relationship with God—and your mentee's relationship with God—are primary and most important. You pattern for your mentee what a relationship with God looks like. Invite them into worship with you. Discuss prayer, study, worship, and emphasize the importance of attending worship services as well as personal spiritual growth habits.

There are multiple tools available for us to study and develop intimacy with God. You may choose to study together or hold each other accountable to further develop these skills. It is important to emphasize that strong leaders depend on the Lord. This dependence is nurtured in our quiet times through study, prayer, and worship.

Out of your intimate relationship with Jesus, direct your friends toward an intimate relationship with Jesus.

Naomi and Ruth

Naomi represents the reluctant mentor. We find her story in the book of Ruth. At first, she is caught in her own pain. She experienced great loss and was hopeless. Her husband died, and her two sons died; she was left with only her two daughters-in-law, and neither of them shared her Israelite heritage. Initially, Ruth appeared to be a burden to her. Take a moment to read Ruth chapter 1. Naomi is distraught. She has no idea how she will care for herself, let alone two daughters-in-law. Her son's wife, Orpah, returns to her own family. But Ruth pledges her life to Naomi and to Naomi's God. Naomi finally agrees.

Throughout the story, we see a change in Naomi. She embraces Ruth and guides her to a good man. Through Ruth's son, the line of David is formed, and through David's line comes Jesus the Messiah. Now that is a happy ending to a story that began tragically. There was no guarantee their story would end this way. But they traveled it together anyway. Life was better for both of them because they were not alone.

Notice that Ruth, the younger, had to plead with Naomi to accept her. Like Ruth, Millennials want to be pursued. They want to be accepted, loved, and wanted by you. Are you reluctant? Have you allowed circumstances to sway you from mentoring? Allow the Holy Spirit to minister to and heal the hurt and reluctance. Is He imploring you to move forward and accept your Ruth?

Once Naomi accepted Ruth, we see Naomi transition into teacher of her culture and society. She is educated in the cultural nuances of the Hebrew people and expertly guided Ruth through them. Remember, Ruth was a foreigner; she needed Naomi. Millennials need your guiding hands in the current cultural conditions. This means you must be aware, informed, and intentional. And you must be aware of the belief systems of the next generation. You do not have to agree with them, but you must be aware.

So…are you willing to be someone's Naomi?

Mordecai and Esther

Mordecai represents the daring mentor. He took great risks for both himself and Esther to get her to a place of powerful influence. Their story is found in the book of Esther.

Israel was in the midst of a desperate time. Held captive by another Kingdom, its future appeared hopeless. Mordecai had raised Esther as his own daughter; he was cunning with his instruction for her not to reveal her heritage when she was taken—allegedly forced—into the king's harem. And through his guidance, Esther became queen. In turn, she was able to save her people—the entire nation of Israel. Courageous beyond her years, she chose to live as Mordecai taught. Esther was challenged, convicted, and perhaps cut to the heart by Mordecai's words—"And who knows but that you have come to your royal position for such a time as this?" (Esther 4:14 NLT).

The danger here is risk for the sake of risk. This was not the case for Mordecai, but our society has bred some intense adrenaline junkies. We encourage risky behavior only when it grows the individual and in turn, God's Kingdom. We need to recognize when it is time to be brave and when to play it safe. I once encouraged a young woman to venture to Africa on a mission trip, while others I have challenged to examine their motivation. Is the risk an answer to God's call, as with Esther, or is it something else? Is it an escape, or an ego booster? If yes, then it needs to be avoided.

Mordecai's wisdom helped Esther survive in a foreign culture. Yours can do the same.

Elijah And Elisha

> You are only human, and the good that happens through you is only from God.

Elijah was the bold mentor. He lived his life as if nothing was impossible. When God spoke, Elijah believed Him, and many miracles happened through Elijah. But he was still human and, like all of us, had his flaws and weak moments. I, for one, am glad Scripture captures these moments as well as the great ones. It reminds us to persevere when our circumstances don't make sense. And it reminds us we are only human, and the good that happens through us is only from God.

When Elijah brought on Elisha, he did not mince words. Elijah spoke and he expected Elisha to respond. We don't see many exchanges between these two men in the Bible. But we do see the results of their relationship as Elisha continued on as Elijah's successor. Read about them in I Kings 19 – II Kings 2.

The bold mentor works well with those who have strong personalities. Bold people do not mince words; they say what they mean and can overpower others. Bold people appear rude when they are actually confident. They know God can accomplish anything so they advise to just follow Him, and they don't handle others' doubt well. Boldness combined with legalism is deadly. These individuals can kill the spirit of others. If you have a bold personality, you must recognize when gentleness is required. Of course you stand on truth, but truth must be delivered with grace. Otherwise you may overwhelm others and they will shut down. Remember—your goal is to build relationship, not crush it.

Have the boldness of Elijah but don't forget compassion and grace in your relationship.

Elizabeth and Mary

Elizabeth represents the encouraging mentor. Oh what she must have done for Mary's spirit when she greeted her with joy! Luke 1:41-42 "When Elizabeth heard Mary's greeting, the baby leaped in her womb, and Elizabeth was filled with the Holy Spirit. In a loud voice she exclaimed: 'Blessed are you among women, and blessed is the child you will bear'" (Luke 1:41-42 NLT)!

Mary's story—betrothed and pregnant of the Holy Spirit—was unfathomable to most people, but not to Elizabeth. Culturally, Mary's pregnancy was social suicide. Although betrothed, she was not yet married. If not for Joseph's brave acceptance of her (as he was instructed to do by an angelic dream), she faced death by stoning.

God prepared Elizabeth to take Mary in and teach her despite the awkward social dynamics of the situation. Elizabeth was a builder of faith for Mary. She reminded Mary of the great responsibility she had been given. Elizabeth lifted the burden of this task and replaced it with exaltation.

I wonder how often Mary thought back to this day, with fond memories I expect. It must have built her faith and allowed her to trust God in times of doubt or fear. Did she hear Elizabeth's voice when she was having a baby in a stable? Did she rely on it when she escaped to Egypt? Did she remember it when she saw her son rejected, beaten, and murdered? I believe she did. Mary had to be a woman of great strength and faith—a foundation Elizabeth helped lay.

Encouraging can be tricky. An encourager can fail if they miss the opportunity to correct. When you speak correction before it will be heard, it falls flat. But it is equally detrimental to never speak correction for fear it may discourage. If you only extend excessive grace, you allow your mentee to stay in sin, enabling them. It is such a fine balance! Do not encourage for the sake of encouragement, but in order to build the other up to follow God's will.

Barnabas—Son of Encouragement

Barnabas means "son of encouragement," but he was also an initiator. Barnabas approached Saul and invited Him into fellowship of the disciples in Jerusalem (Acts 9:27). He showed Saul hospitality, and Saul grew in faith and knowledge during this time. Later, Barnabas again invited Saul to go with him to Antioch (Acts 11:25), where they taught together for a year. Look at the power of this initiated relationship. Barnabas befriended Saul when no one else would. Saul, whose name eventually changed to Paul, went on to write a good portion of the New Testament.

The problem with initiators is they don't always follow through. They can start a relationship but can become inconsistent. This can be disheartening to anyone but it is particularly to the millennial generation—it adds to their suspicion. Trust is not given until it is earned. Consistent behavior and committed pattern wins them over.

Paul and Timothy

Paul (formerly Saul) represents the teacher-mentor. He spent a great deal of time teaching Timothy the Scriptures. Timothy was previously taught by his mother and grandmother, so he was well-versed in the Old Testament. Paul saw Timothy's potential and continued building onto the foundation that was there. This is a delightful relationship—truly one that developed into a father-son bond. I love the encouragement he shared that has stimulated maturity in the young throughout history—"Don't let anyone think less of you because you are young. Be an example to all believers in what you say, in the way you live, in your love, your faith, and your purity" (I Timothy 4:12 NLT).

The trick with being a teacher-mentor is to not do all the talking. I'll readily admit I love to talk. I love to teach. Don't you want to listen to me

> Be an active, reflective listener.

all the time? No, you don't! Mentees need time to process what is already in their head. They have multiple resources to learn from, but they need a safe place to digest their knowledge. You can be that safe place. Be an active, reflective listener. Help them define and refine their opinions. Make them think! That is a sign of a good teacher.

Paul met this challenge and his words ring true with us today.

"As apostles of Christ we certainly had a right to make some demands of you, but instead we were like children among you. Or we were like a mother feeding and caring for her own children. We loved you so much that we shared with you not only God's Good News but our own lives, too" (I Thessalonians 2:7-8 NLT).

You are motivated by love and share your life for the purpose of God's Good News—the Gospel.

Anyone Can Do It

To whom do you most relate? Any person can mentor, as Scripture reflects in these examples. Did you see yourself in any of them?

I see myself more like Elizabeth with a dash of Paul. I have to guard myself against giving disingenuous encouragement—it's worthless if it is not accurate. In addition, I need to recognize when to keep my mouth closed and actively engage in listening. My brain needs to engage in what they are saying, and not just what I'm planning to say next.

Self-awareness is key. Do you know your strengths? Are you aware of your weaknesses? Can you entrust both to the Holy Spirt and move forward in this journey?

God designed you; your personality is birthed in His creation. If you seek Him, He will nurture your passion. He will empower you to mentor and lead you to the right people. Psalm 139 says, "You saw me before I was born. Every day of my life was recorded in your book. Every moment was laid out before a single day had passed" (Psalm 139:16 NLT). Tap into God

> God designed you; your personality is birthed in His creation.

and see your design as He sees it. He likes what He put in you. He sees it as good (Genesis 1:31).

All mentors share a surrendered heart. You must learn to pray, What do you have for me today Lord? He prepares you and He works with your design. After all, He is the designer. Choose God's will over yours, as the writer of Psalm 40 did: "I take joy in doing your will, my God, for your instructions are written on my heart" (Psalm 40:8 NLT).

You are not alone in this process. The Holy Spirit directs you—that is good news! You don't have to have it figured out; you must trust He is in control. Romans 8:9 (NLT) "But you are not controlled by your sinful nature. You are controlled by the Spirit if you have the Spirit of God living in you." Take steps of faith that are yielded to God; you will find your way. God gives wisdom—sound judgment. But we are directed to ask for it. Trust you are moving in the right direction until the Holy Spirit's instruction tells you otherwise.

It's All Good!

Scripture says God works everything for His good. God is the author of the phrase, "it's all good!" If we act according to His purpose, Romans 8:38 says, He will make it good. "And we know that God causes everything to work together for the good of those who love God and are called according to his purpose for them" (Romans 8:28 NLT). Even if you misstep—which you will from time to time—a life surrendered to God will move in His direction. First nurture your relationship with Jesus and then take a step forward in mentoring. If you are not sure, take a step anyway. Either direction is a step of faith. God promises to turn even your mistakes for good if you seek after Him.

> Love is communicated through sharing lives together.

Each of these Biblical examples were empowered by the Holy Spirit. I cannot say this enough. We need

God's lead and power to live these relationships. It is not because it is always difficult but it is important to be connected directly to the power source. Mentors influence and build the church. With Jesus' direction you are building His Kingdom. You are doing His will "on earth as it is in heaven." With the power of the Holy Spirit you develop a sense of family with those God has brought into your life. He will deliver the wisdom you need to encourage the next generation. This family bond is rooted in His love.

Love is communicated through sharing lives together. Our pluralistic society sends continual mixed messages of relative truth to our young people. You are their sounding board, a safe place to reflect what they learn. Listen, reflect, and give them a safe place to sort out their lives. Ask questions to provoke thought or guide the conversation, but never force. This generation will find a way through any available crack if pushed into a corner. They do not respond well to unyielding opinions. It does not mean you cannot have strong opinions, on the contrary—you should have grounded beliefs in multiple areas. But your opinions must be delivered with the fruit of the Spirit, not with legalism, fear, or hatred. Everything you do and say should be rooted in love.

This generation is under a great deal of pressure to have their life figured out. Society has subtly told them they need to be smarter, more efficient, and more daring then the previous generation:

Don't settle. Follow your passions, and change the world! How, you ask? Oh that is up to you! No one can tell you how to live your life! But remember you are only young once so get it right.

That is a lot of pressure, isn't it? Pressure can crush a youthful spirit when they feel they have to go it alone. It stops them in their tracks, not because they don't want to move forward but simply because they don't know how to move forward. The daily grind wears at their resolve to reach for higher goals.

But the pressure isn't just in the secular culture. Current Christian culture also comes with pressure. It stresses God has a plan and a purpose for each one, individually created to fulfill God's will in His Kingdom. While this can inspire them to pursue their passions, it can also freeze them in their tracks, shine a light on their insecurities, raising questions like What if I make a mistake? Or, What if I miss God's plan? Or worse, belief statements: I see no purpose. I must be flawed, damaged, or broken. God can't use me.

I'm sure you've even felt the anxiety and pressure. It's exponentially compounded for the next generation. You are there to relieve the pressure, to remind them of what they have already accomplished and where they are headed. You are there to give them shoulders to stand on so they can see above the crowd. This is a long-term commitment meant to guide and launch them into their purpose. It is not a passive relationship, it is not a pressured relationship. It is a truth-based, guiding, and wildly loving relationship.

How My Dad Changed My Life

When I was in college, I intended to go into genetic research. It was cutting-edge science; new discoveries were made daily. They were mapping the human genome and it fascinated me. Then I started my research; I worked for a Professor whose work explored pleiotropic inheritance, which is where one gene influences multiple traits in an individual. Here's the problem: I was always alone in the lab. This extroverted girl needed people!

So my dad suggested I become a teacher. My first thought was, "I didn't like teenagers when I was one. I certainly don't want to spend the rest of my life with them!" Apparently, I needed some maturing. With my boredom in the lab and stress in the classroom, I knew I had to make a change. I remember struggling through my Advanced Genetics midterm, certain I failed. This was the final straw, and I switched my major as soon as I left the exam. Later, I found out I had gotten a B on the exam, and that the professor had forgotten to teach an entire section he tested us over, so he curved the grades. But for me, the deed was done. I added the Biology Education major because I didn't know what else to do. When I made that decision, I had no idea the impact it would have on the rest of my life. I thought it was a temporary solution until I figured out what I was called to do, but it turned into my life's passion. Where would I be if I had not taken that first step? If my dad had not suggested a move?

I believe now that was a God-directed step. This is where He wanted me.

Build Your Legacy

Do not let fear keep you or your mentee from moving forward. Mistakes will happen but progress will not happen without risk. It is better to risk and fail then to stay in the same place your entire life. This is a wasted life. This is not a life of impact.

Look at what it can do. Saul, for example, Saul did not become Paul at his conversion. In general, the church was afraid of Saul. But not Barnabas. Barnabas brought Saul into the church where he was mentored. Then he became Paul. Paul, a now developed believer of Christ, in turn reached out to Mark, Silas, and then Timothy. Do you see the importance of each generation blessing the next?

This is how the church grows—by making disciples. We, the body of Christ, are the product of the early church discipleship. And we keep producing more churches, more disciples. We do not just bring them to Jesus, we nurture their relationship with Him. We must continue this pattern of discipleship if we want the Church to survive and thrive.

Are you up for the challenge? Can you extend yourself as our Biblical examples did? Can you share your life and look for spiritual children? Are you willing to lean into the Holy Spirit and let Him guide you in this adventure? This generation is all around you. You need to take the initiative. Here is your first step: say hello to every person you see at church under 30 years old. Do you feel invisible to them? You are not. They are waiting. Build your legacy.

Dear Father, Thank you for designing me in a unique fashion. Help me to remember who I am in you. Help me to live authentically in the personality you gave me. Make me aware of my gifts and flaws. Teach me to embrace and understand the way I relate to others. Give me eyes to see those that fit me. In Jesus' Name, AMEN!

Questions:

1. List the mentor personalities sited from scripture. Check the ones that you identify with.

2. After reading this chapter, what strengths do you see in yourself? What weaknesses?

3. How can you utilize your strengths in mentoring?

4. How do we deliver our opinions with the fruit of the Spirit (Galatians 5:22)?

5. What is stopping you from mentoring? Pray for God's guidance.

Chapter Five: Connected

Climb the dunes. That was our goal. On a summer visit to Northern Michigan, a stop at Sleeping Bear Dunes National Lakeshore is a must. It is pristine land and my daughters wanted nothing more than to hike the trail from the parking lot to Lake Michigan. Four miles roundtrip doesn't sound bad—except for the fact that it is all sand. Oh, and the hike to the lake is mostly uphill. Needless to say, it's not a hike for wimps.

Was I up for this? I knew on my own there was no way I would attempt such a trek. But together—now that was somewhat imaginable. So up we went. We encouraged each other, joked about the work out, and enjoyed the beauty of the forest and the sand and the water. Four miles later, when we finally made it back to the car—and in one piece, even—we congratulated each other on our accomplishment. The journey was worth it because we did it together. Together. We connected with each other on a totally new level—literally, because

Scripture instructs to love one another, serve one another, and share with one another. One Savior, one heartbeat. One unbreakable bond.

the dunes are almost 500 feet above the lake. But also because it was a new experience, and at times, challenging for all of us. But it connected us all.

Admit it—you crave connection. Relationships are the core of community—a local neighborhood community, an office community, a sports team, and of course, a church. But even in the midst of these communities existing all around us, it's true that living a life that nourishes fellowship goes against our society. Americans cherish independence. Consumerism drives our lifestyle (I'm looking at you, Black Friday!). Self-focused, we choose involvement based on our own needs, and often, the need for connection and the desire for autonomy clash.

But. Scripture calls the Church to be in community. Scripture instructs to love one another, serve one another, and share with one another. Connection. Yes, church is counter-cultural. Jesus regularly and radically challenged the status quo.

The church is a living organism, not a destination. It is called the Body of Christ, where everything is connected, and every "body part" is necessary. (See I Corinthians 12.) We need each other, or else we won't all function fully and properly. We must all be connected. This kind of connection makes the church a unique place of community.

Be The Church

Friend, can I ask you a question? Are you a member of a local church? I mean, more than just attending once a week? To be honest, church attendance in itself is a poor substitute for true fellowship—true connection. Being committed to a church is actually biblical—did you know that? Attendance and involvement is actually the first step to connection and community. Look at what Hebrews 10 says:

"And let us not neglect our meeting together, as some people do, but encourage one another, especially now that the day of his return is drawing near" (Hebrews 10:25 NLT).

May I ask you another question? If your normal Sunday morning doesn't involve church, why not? You need this biblical foundation to support you as you move into any God-centered action. The early church—those committed to the message of Jesus shortly after He returned to Heaven after His time here on earth—lived in community. They had the connection thing down. They shared their very lives with each other (see Acts 2:42). They gave to each other when someone needed something. They met together in homes. They connected with each other. They fellowshipped together. And the church grew.

I encourage you to search out a place that will become a home for you. The size of the church does not matter, nor the type of music they use or what kind of clothes they typically wear. Look for a place that has a heart in sync with the Bible and your own heart. One Savior, one heartbeat. One unbreakable bond.

"A person standing alone can be attached and defeated, but two can stand back-to-back and conquer. Three are even better, for a triple-braided cord is not easily broken" (Ecclesiastes 4:12 NLT).

Please don't misunderstand: yes, we can belong to organizations outside of our church. We are to love people whether they go to your church or not. But the question is: are you sacrificing one for the other? Think about it, where is your time invested? There are many wonderful organizations that you can be a part of. But Jesus calls us to build His church. Is your time investment paying off for the Kingdom of God?

Unlike other organizations which revolve around good and charitable causes, the church revolves around Jesus and His message. It is the core of why the church meets.

Before moving on to some of the benefits of community and connection, let's look at what an ideal church community might look like as described in Scripture.

Psalm 15 (NIV) A psalm of David.

"Lord, who may dwell in your sacred tent? Who may live on your holy mountain? The one whose walk is blameless, who does what is righteous, who speaks the truth from their heart; whose tongue utters no slander, who does no wrong to a neighbor, and casts no slur on others; who despises a vile person but honors those who fear the Lord; who keeps an oath even when it hurts, and does not change their mind; who lends money to the poor without interest; who does not accept a bribe against the innocent. Whoever does these things will never be shaken."

Well, what do you think? Do you qualify? No? Don't feel bad—Psalm 15:2 counts us all out. "Those whose walk is blameless..." If we're all honest with ourselves, none of us are blameless.

Do we fail? Yes, sometimes abysmally. We are accused of hypocrisy because often it is true. We struggle to be true to ourselves, yet fear others will see our faults. It's a narrow road we walk, accompanied by deep ditches on either side. One ditch is legalism, the other is permissiveness. Oh, the balance we must maintain!

And it is true that sometimes, churches fail. Sometimes Jesus—the very core of The Church—is forgotten, and His message is taken over by politics, policy, and sometimes even doctrine. They overshadow the simple truth that the church is the family of God, and as family members, we are to reflect His character.

We do fail, but we are only human. We still mess up, we still make mistakes, though it is unfortunate some huge mistakes are made by those proclaiming Jesus. We are not perfect and don't claim to be.

But we all have Jesus. And when we live in community—in connection—with each other, we work to sand off those rough edges, to push each other toward Jesus and a greater life, living and walking as members of God's family.

We live righteous lives only through His empowerment. Our human temptations to lie, gossip, put down, break vows, and ignore the poor hit us every day. But it is easier when we have others to encourage us and hold us accountable. When we fail, we seek forgiveness. When others fail, we extend it. This is what helps us stay blameless.

Thank you, Lord, for Jesus, the Holy Spirit, and community to help us reflect You better!

A House Unified for Glory

We, as a collective people, are God's very temple. The book of Revelation describes a wonderful scene: "I heard a loud shout from the throne, saying, 'Look, God's home is now among his people! He will live with them, and they will be his people. God himself will be with them'" (Revelation 21:3, NLT). Though John is describing an event to happen in the future, it's encouraging to know God is looking forward to the time when we can be together forever. What a privilege we are given! God is Holy and He chose to set us apart so He can dwell in us (I Corinthians 6). We need to face this with reverence. It humbles me and reminds me of my inadequacies. BUT Jesus is our gateway.

Think about it. Jesus came to the earth—He gave up heaven to live on earth like us. He was fully God and fully human. As a baby, He entered the world, humble, tiny, and vulnerable. He grew. He ministered. He died a brutal death, took on my sin and your sin, and rose again. All for you and I to have eternal life. Are you in awe? I'm having a mini church service as I type! Thank you Jesus! Words escape me. You, Lord, are beautiful!

God's glory dwells in you. Make room for it to shine on others daily. Community is designed to nurture and encourage this in each other. It's truly beautiful!

I recently returned from a trip to North Carolina, where we visited a church rocked by racial hate crimes. The church had been partially destroyed by arson. At dinner, I realized the significance of our time there, and the power of community in that church. The pastors received our love as well as service and gifts; prayer and physical presence brought encouragement. Such simple acts will reverberate throughout their community as they are renewed to do what God called them to do. It was the easiest mission trip I've ever participated in, yet, it was full of impact.

Sometimes, my friend, it is the little acts.

Jesus declared and even prayed for us to live as one, a unified whole.

> Unity drives growth and effectiveness of God's Kingdom.

"I pray that they will all be one, just as you and I are one—as you are in me, Father, and I am in you. And may they be in us so that the world will believe you sent me" (John 17:21, NLT). Community produces unity. It's even part of the word itself! Unity drives growth and effectiveness of God's Kingdom. Your union with God and each other draws others to us. It is a beautiful thing to see the Body of Christ work together. "How good and pleasant it is when God's people live together in unity" (Psalm 133:1 NIV)!

Unity is the goal. We need to stop our criticism of one another and nurture the common ground. If the church is fighting with itself, how are we going to attract others to Jesus? God's love brings unity, not quarreling. How we live together as the church declares a message to the world. It should be one of Jesus and His love.

Crafting Your Coffee Klatch

You need a group of friends you can rely on. Some call it a posse or squad but that doesn't really work for me. I'm not a horse-riding, law-enforcing kind of woman. I prefer the term "coffee klatch." "Klatch" is a German word meaning to gather for light conversation or gossip. Throughout history, women have gathered together to exchange tidbits of their lives with one another. But often we have preferred to exchange tidbits of other peoples' lives with one another. That' a problem.

We've got to redeem the definition and perception of such a group, especially with a definition like that. But let's talk about that for a moment. Women seem to have a natural propensity for gossip. Friend, we must be aware of it and avoid it at all costs. Scripture instructs to steer clear of it (see Ephesians 4:25-32). If you're not sure you have permission to say something, don't.

Years ago, I was at a public event. My friend and I saw a sports celebrity she had worked with in an advertising campaign. She then began to share the difficulties she experienced working with him. I then shared something I had observed at another event. We exchanged a few more comments, both of us made others around us aware that we were in the know. We didn't actually know the man personally, but we had experienced him firsthand. Then it happened. We were interrupted by another woman. It turned out to be his wife. Talk about an awkward moment! Embarrassed, we continued on in silence, down what felt like a never ending staircase.

Friend, please learn from my mistake. We spoke about situations that were true but not ours to share and it was hurtful to others around us. Scripture is clear: gossip in any form is wrong.

Your coffee klatch should be a place to share your heart, not a place to share rumors and idle talk. Build relationships within your home church for support and strength. We are such relational beings.

People that "get" us are precious. They are safe. Be that precious person for someone.

So, how do you build a safe, godly coffee klatch? Well, first let me clear something up: this is not about the coffee. I make this suggestion to women and their first response is "I don't drink coffee." That is not the point. Socializing with like minded women is the focus. You decide your common interest. Your "coffee klatch" could be a book club, Bible Study, or a running group. But make sure you do more than the activity: purpose to support one another.

My coffee klatch is the Dragonfly Ministry. These are the women who believe in God's call in this ministry. They offer their gifts and prayer support to see God move. It encourages me and humbles me. It relieves what can be a lonely burden of leadership. It is a gift to know I am not alone.

The women who support me don't necessarily meet together. They are the individual women I trust with my inner thoughts. One of these women is my walking buddy, and she is my true safe place. With her I share ideas, vent frustrations, and rejoice over blessings. She is interested in my well-being and I am invested in hers. There is beauty in a trusted friendship. A place, where confidences are shared and kept, is treasured. This is the type of friendship community fosters. Do you long for this kind of friendship? Be this kind of friend.

> It is only in true, pure genuine community we can begin to understand the mystery of God.

Paul encouraged community in the book of Colossians, his letter to the church in Colossae. Paul wrote, "I want them to be encouraged and knit together by strong ties of love. I want them to have complete confidence that they understand God's mysterious plan, which is Christ himself. In him lie hidden all the treasures of wisdom and knowledge" (Colossians 2:2-3 NLT). The words Paul used here are strong. He refers to deep inner ties, which include unity and strength. Examine the Greek words used and you will see his description refers to deep inner ties; one that implies unity and strength. The unconditional love implied here is rooted in Jesus himself. These deep ties lead to a comprehension of Jesus. It is only in true, pure genuine community we can begin to understand the mystery of God. Isn't that marvelous?

Your klatch is a living organism. It changes over time. People may move in and out. There may be times when a person has a need and later has the opportunity to give. It is not an exclusive group or a clique, but a more intentional purposeful community. Your klatch should nurture the fruit of the Spirit, so you each grow in love, joy, peace, patience, faithfulness, gentleness, goodness, kindness, and self-control.

But your klatch does not just support the good parts of you. Real friends will support your authenticity; genuine friends see your real self. The vulnerability you share, however raw it may be, allows you to be your true self. Real friends want your true self; they know your true self is more attractive than a masked version. Find friends who won't let you hide.

Bringing Life Through Real Friendship

Jesus made His purpose clear: to bring life. The Holy Spirit resides in us to nurture life in us as well as in those around us. Jesus said, "The Spirit alone gives eternal life. Human effort accomplishes nothing. And the very words I have spoken to you are spirit and life" (John 6:63, NLT). In community, you connect to love others toward that life—not with your own power but with God's.

I have to be honest, though: there's a certain amount of messiness in life-giving community. You and I are are human, and we make mistakes. We won't always get along perfectly. You will get offended, but you need to not stay offended. People are offensive, either deliberately or thoughtlessly, but the source doesn't really matter. But the only choice is to forgive. Yes, you are to confront the offender—that is biblical. (See Matthew 18.) However, your forgiveness does not rest on the other person's response. It is rooted in your love of Jesus: He forgave, so you forgive. Do not hold onto offenses.

Does this make you a doormat? Should you allow people to walk on you to get what they want? No, but you also shouldn't protect yourself and in the process forego fellowship. Unforgiveness and bitterness hardens your heart. As you meet together, especially if you are in a leadership position, you need tough skin and a soft heart. See offensive behavior as the short falls of the other person instead of personal attacks. It's true you cannot please everyone but you can love everyone. This is an interesting dynamic of community. Difficult people need love. Pray for them. Ask God to give you His eyes for that person. Take a break if you must but don't shut them out.

It is true there are life-sucking people out there—those who, for various reasons, have convinced themselves they absolutely need to control other people. In their presence everything is about them and their issues. Stop right there. Not everyone with problems—even extensive problems—is a life sucker. In every relationship there is give-and-take. Sometimes you have to give more, and sometimes you need more. Sometimes you need sympathy, while other times you seek answers. There's nothing wrong with either, but individuals who do not know this balance continue to drain the energy from those around them. It becomes a problem, a self-inflicted trap, when a person's identity becomes entangled in their issues. They look to people to sustain their life instead of Jesus. You aren't their Savior—Jesus is. You must direct these individuals back to Him. Jesus came for our freedom, not entanglement to self or sin—"So if the Son sets you free, you are truly free" (John 8:36 NLT).

But it's also important to recognize this in ourselves, too. Self-evaluation. Am I sucking the life out of those around me? Here's the test: who do you talk about most? Do you always talk about yourself? If you do, you might not realize it. No one wants to be selfish or self-focused, though innately, we are exactly that. Listen to the conversation the next time you gather with close friends. It's okay to talk about yourself, adding your experience to the conversation. But the question is—are you talking only about yourself?

If you're feeling particularly brave, ask for friends' input. This is not a time to beat yourself up, just a time to learn about yourself and to become more Christlike. Confess selfishness to your friends, and ask them to pray for you and hold you accountable. Let them know your others-focused goal.

Or you may find the opposite to be true—you never talk about yourself. Are you unwilling to share? Why? Some people are more guarded than others, and it's okay to be private. But it's a concern if you are afraid of vulnerability. Find a safe friend to share your heart—it doesn't have to be a whole group of friends. This can be scary if past friends have hurt you. But a dangerously guarded heart will not receive new friends. Just one friend starts this process. You only need to share a little at a time: build trust and find freedom. Real friendship.

Klatch = Connection = Sanctification

Your klatch is more than just a group of friends sharing your heart and life with. Your klatch is a place of connection, a place of support, and place for you to grow in sanctification. These women keep you accountable. But it's also a great place to test ideas. You can ask questions like "I think God has called me to _____. What do you think?" Weigh their answers, and ask the Holy Spirit to share wisdom through these friends. Your friends can be an avenue to hear the Lord's direction for you.

Your klatch can also be a place to express doubt. Recently, I shared a fear with one of my klatch friends. Soon, I will need to invest cash into the ministry to accomplish the next goal. The problem is it is not a set amount of money. What if I don't have enough? What if I'm not hearing God correctly and I am wasting His resources? I expected my friend to commiserate with me. Something like; "that must be tough" or even "you might want to rethink that." Instead she said, "Now, you know you are called to do this. Go for it and trust God will provide." It wasn't what I expected to hear, but it was what I need to hear. It was exactly what I needed to have the courage to risk it. These are the kind of friends we need.

Your klatch is a place of support, not only emotionally, but actual physical support. Like in Exodus 17, when Moses needed help with his arms—literally. Moses sent Joshua into battle, while he stood above on a hill with his arms raised in prayer and worship to God. As his arms grew tired and fell, Joshua lost ground in the battle. So Aaron and Hur then came to Moses' aid. They literally held up Moses arms until the battle was over. Sometimes this is the kind of support you need. Sometimes you're on the frontline in ministry, like Joshua, fighting battles that you can't win on your own. Sometimes you're praying in intercession, like Moses. And sometimes, you're supporting the supporter like Aaron and Hur!

Whatever you're doing, and whoever you are, you're needed, and you need others. You draw emotional and physical strength from the unity and support of your klatch.

Correction is another important part of your klatch. Like we talked a few pages ago about sharing the conversation, you need friends who will tell you when you might be too much. You need people in your life that will expose your flaws. Whether those are imperfections in your character or an errant plan, you need people who will speak truth in love.

"As iron sharpens iron, so a friend sharpens a friend" (Proverbs 27:17 NLT). You want and need people that will smooth your rough edges. The key is listening when they do. A genuine friend does not criticize because they are critical. A genuine friend corrects because they want the best for you. Repeating criticism could mean your friend is actually a bully, but it also might mean you didn't listen the first time.

> A genuine friend corrects because they want the best for you.

The prophet Nathan and King David had this kind of relationship. David committed multiple sins in his adulterous relationship with Bathsheba, culminating with the murder of Uriah, Bathsheba's husband. David was caught up in his own trap. But he was the king, and nobody wants to step in and correct the king. Thankfully, he had Nathan in his court. Nathan confronted David and David repented. Yes, the damage was done but Nathan put an end to it further damage, and pushed David toward a righteous reconciliation. You can read their story in I Samuel 12.

You need a Nathan.

Rushing Water

At the center of your klatch should be none other than the Holy Spirit. Jesus sent His Holy Spirit to inhabit us. Not only does the Holy Spirit help you in your weaknesses (Romans 6) and produce fruit in you (Galatians 5), the Holy Spirit nourishes and waters your relationships with the living water Jesus promised: "Anyone who believes in me may come and drink! For the Scriptures declare, 'Rivers of living water will flow from his heart'" (John 7:38-39 NLT). When Jesus said "living water," he was speaking about the Spirit, who would be given to everyone believing in him. (The Spirit had not yet been given, because Jesus had not yet returned to Heaven.)

But think about water with me for a moment. Living water flows. Water that doesn't flow becomes stagnate, inhibiting life. But flowing water births life. Which would you rather drink from—a river or a pond? A river, of course. The water in a river moves, keeping it clean, but a stagnate pond just sits, collecting all sorts of unlovely things. Stagnate water brings disease and death. But flowing water brings life. Jesus says the Holy Spirit is water that is both flowing and living. Worship, paired with relationships in the Holy Spirit, facilitate the flow of this living water. At church, you worship through song and the message, filling you with the Holy Spirit. But without interaction through relationships, that water becomes stagnate. Church attendance without relationships dams the water.

Paul, too, wrote of a type water flow in his letter to the Philippians. He spoke of his life as another kind of water flow—a "liquid offering." He says, "But I will rejoice even if I lose my life, pouring it out like a liquid offering to God, just like your faithful service is an offering to God. And I want all of you to share that joy" (Philippians 2:17, NLT). Paul describes his life of service as a type of water flow, with a sole purpose of serving others for God. Take in so you can pour out; become full so that you may pour out. All you have is to serve others. Live life in this manner and let this become your reputation.

For years, this knowledge was tucked away in my heart. Over time it became part of my life; it was not just what I knew, it became part of who I am. Anyone who participates in Bible Studies and allows God's Word to infiltrate their heart and life will see changes in themselves. You study the Bible to better understand God; you delve into His word to know Him. And when you know the Lord, you do His work. But not only does it affect your character, it is to be used to care for those around you. You reach a time when you've been fed enough that it has to come out somewhere.

Let it. Others in your life observe you, and I'm talking about more people than just those you mentor. I'm not saying you're being stalked, but people are aware of those who actively serve. Think about it—you know exactly who it is in your church who serves consistently, and who doesn't. People notice. Why does this matter? Your status in the community actually determines your approachability. People want to serve with good people, and your friends reflect your character. Proverbs says,

"Though good advice lies deep within the heart, a person with understanding will draw it out. Many will say they are loyal friends, but who can find one who is truly reliable? The godly walk with integrity; blessed are their children who follow them" (Proverbs 20:5-7 NLT).

People are watching you; they're seeing how you get filled with the Spirit's living water and how it gets poured out. The individuals you may want to mentor are seeing all of this. Bless those who observe you and those who follow you.

So—how's your water? Is there a dam or is it flowing freely and bringing life? Do you feel stagnate? Break the dam and let it flow. Initiate friendships. Risk rejection. You have so much to give. The living water in you has its own flavor, and intermingled with others in relationship, it becomes rich and quenches your soul. When the Holy Spirit mixes all our flavors together, community is born.

Whose life does yours flow into? Where do you pour out your living water and invest the love you are freely given? Don't keep it to yourself, letting it become stagnate. Build a network of waterways around you, where living water flows back and forth and then out into your community. The Holy Spirit is the source of this living water, but we can—and must—share that source with others. You bring refreshment to your world when you truly live in community as the church. You pour into your klatch and in turn, to others we meet throughout the day. True fellowship fills you and you overflow, pouring into others.

Dear Lord, help each of us to build a community. Knit us together. Give us people we can trust and encourage. Show us how to work in a way that builds your Kingdom. Connect us together with those You bring into our lives. In Jesus' Name, AMEN.

Questions:

1. Where are you connected?

2. Do you feel you belong to a community at your church? Why or why not?

3. What does the phrase "Jesus is our gateway" mean in reference to God's temple?

4. How does community produce unity?

5. Do you have a "klatch?" If not, who would you like to build a friendship with? Invite her to join you in a common interest.

6. Did you take time to reflect on "life-sucker" traits? Do you share too much? Do you share too little?

7. Who do you pour into?

Chapter 6 — Meet Some Millennials

I'm guessing you've already heard a lot about the Millennial Generation—they're lazy, entitled, and still living in mom and dad's basement and working at Starbucks, right? Well, there's a lot more to these young adults than just the stereotype.

I wanted to give these young adults in the Millennial Generation a voice in this book, since it's all about mentoring them. My hope is through their words you will experience God's love for His children, and hear the heart cry of the future church—actually, our current church. My hope is their words will inspire you to step forward and build them up, encourage them with your experience, and simply invest in them and see God's Kingdom flourish.

So, I asked them what they wanted the world to know about their generation. Here's a glimpse into the hearts of some of my Millennial friends.

What Do You Want The World To Know About Your Generation?

"We are really good at acting like we have it all together, but often when we say 'it's okay,' what we really mean is 'life is falling apart but I don't want to bother anyone with my problems.' Also, we may act like we know it all, but we don't. At least for me, I really need the guidance of the older women in the church so I can become who Christ wants me to be." – Caitlin, 24

"That even though our generation doesn't seem to care with all that the materialistic things the world has to offer, there is a good mass of us who still do, and are working to change the world in Christ's name as we speak. There are some of us who want to unite together, regardless of race, age, Christian denominations and the factors set aside to change the world for God." – Lauren, 23

"Just because we go about things differently and value certain things (like self-expression) higher than our parent's generations, it doesn't mean our ideas are bad or that we don't take life and responsibility seriously." – Annie, 24

"We are creative and passionate but lack direction. We love all the opportunities we have but are overwhelmed by all the possibilities." – Mark, 22

"Just because you've met one person in my generation doesn't mean you've met us all. We are individuals, with our own opinions, work ethics, and dreams. Don't assume you know what we're thinking, because when you do, you drive a wedge between us." – Christina, 26

"I would have to say that I would want the world to know that my generation is hard working and ready to step up to the plate!" – Jessica, 22

"I would want the world to know that our generation is not made up of mindless technology zombies as we are usually portrayed, but hard-working individuals ready to be taken seriously for our ideas." – Amber, 23

"We are the last generation that isn't afraid to get our hands dirty." – Matt, 31

"I want the world to know that my generation cares. We care about the world and other people. I feel like most older people write us off as "too immature" and they don't really listen to what we have to say." – Elizabeth, 19

"I guess what I want people to know about my generation is that we have a lot of growing to do. I mean look. We are all so glued to our phones, even myself at times, that we forget to enjoy the things in life we did before electronics took over. You know what I mean? There are so many things to do! Girls always post on Facebook and Twitter about what their goals in life are or 'relationship goals' and it's all these pictures of couples out hiking and going on vacation and horseback riding. But what are generating doesn't understand is that you can actually go do those things. Instead we just imagine what it's all like. We daydream about all these goals but our generation doesn't put effort into it. Effort has died. I miss when we were kids. We actually went and walked to our friend's house and socialized. Socialization has turned into social networking. There's no talking, only tweeting.

Maybe I was only supposed to put something positive—lol—but recently there hasn't been anything. I mean we have come great advances in technology but it's also taken over ourselves. Our generation to me, myself included, is we have a lot of growing up to do. We look at this generation that's growing up as ten year-olds with iPhones and we look at them negatively when we are who they look up to! We are a terrible influence." – Taylor, 22

"I want people to know that my generation now understands why our parents said 'no' when we wanted to hear 'yes.' We understand that they wanted to protect us from such harmful and evil things in the world." – Brandis, 28

"It's a tough question. I don't usually think about generations linearly. Culture can be shaped by its circumstance, but every date is still relevant. There is a big emphasis within every generation to talk about character differences. People might not have locked their doors back in the day, but I still think we are all, more or less, similar. I would imagine people are just as good now as they were in the turn of the century. If anything has changed, I would say it's our own personal epiphany that we are good for the world and God has something in us unique and worth displaying. All that to say, I would like for our generation to be known as intergenerational, that they had meaningful relationships with generations above and below their own, and that communities were connected to each other by the rise of God's love and by the desire to have a family." – Alec, 20

Are you listening? Do you see the incredible potential here? Just like you and me, they need encouragement to press on.

Chapter Seven: Why Mentor?

I started this book with a bit of my story—about how I was mentored by Elizabeth and the huge impact she had in my life. I am so grateful for my friendship with Elizabeth!

When I knew I was called to mentoring—that I wanted to be someone else's Elizabeth, I wasn't sure where to start, and I didn't even know what mentoring fully meant. I was nervous. I was scared. I was nervous. I wanted them to like me. I wanted them to think I was cool. I wanted them to know I was hip! (Do people say that anymore? Hip?) Did I mention I was nervous?

But I knew those things were all well-worth the end goal: advancing the Kingdom of Heaven. I knew my feelings of fear and anxiety had to be put away before I could be an Elizabeth for someone else. I didn't know exactly how it was going to happen, and I wasn't even sure what mentoring really was. I just knew I had to step out in faith.

My first attempt at reaching out was somewhat awkward. I invited Christina to join me at a women's event at our church, and I bought her ticket. I don't know why, but the $15 ticket seemed like a big risk at the time. What if she didn't show up? Would my money be wasted? True, I was on a budget, but really? My fear was so misplaced.

Christina did show up. She spent the day with me. We watched the Women of Faith simulcast, joined in during discussion time, and ate lunch together. It was a good day. At the end she asked me to be her mentor. I wasn't sure what she meant but I said yes anyway. This is where my adventure began. How was I supposed to help her? What were the first steps?

Later that month Christina and I met for lunch. I had no agenda because I wasn't sure what I was doing. I started the conversation with a simple question. "What are your expectations of me?" This is where it began. She shared her specific goals and we went from there. It didn't always go smoothly but I pursued the relationship anyway. I have learned a great deal since then. I'm thankful I said yes.

Hope for the Future

"I hope I have room for dessert after this great meal."

"I hope I get the job."

"I hope it doesn't rain tomorrow."

> If you are reading this, God's plan for you is mentoring.

We casually hope for all sorts of things, don't we? Some are benign and some are life changing, but we use the word hope all the time. Hope is even the precursor for faith, but it goes deeper than just a word of favorable uncertainty. In fact, it is the opposite: hope is the expectation for a certain result. Keyword: certain.

And hope is why we mentor.

We have a hope embedded in the next generation for the future of the Church. If you are reading this, God's plan for you is mentoring. It is your responsibility to mentor for the sake—for the hope—of the Church.

Do you agree? Do you feel your passion rise for the next generation? My prayer is the Holy Spirit is inspiring you as you read.

Jeremiah 29:11 is a frequently quoted verse at my church: "'For I know the plans I have for you,' declares the Lord, 'plans to prosper you and not to harm you, plans to give you hope and a future'" (NIV). It is used when new beginnings are examined, like New Years and graduations, and sermons for these events are peppered with it.

But this verse took on a whole new meaning for me recently. My pastor used it in a message, and I thought something along the lines as "oh here we go again…same old verse used every year for a new year." I'm sure the Holy Spirit got a chuckle out of that, right before He said, "Here you go little one, look at it from this angle." There it was—a new twist on this very old promise. The words jumped out at me; I knew the Lord was telling me "These young people are YOUR HOPE and YOUR FUTURE. Through them I will build my Kingdom here on earth as it is in heaven."

Oh how this delights me! The idea that God would allow me to influence others for the continuation of His Kingdom is breathtaking, don't you think? A call to this mission is beautiful!

> Seek after Jesus with your whole self and God will fulfill His promise.

As we read further in Jeremiah 29 we see God calls us to give our whole heart. Unguarded, we hand it over to Him. I know, I know, this is a rather vulnerable position to be in. However, I assure you there is no safer place for your heart than in the hands of God. He is our security and our stronghold (Psalm 18:2). Seek after Jesus with your whole self and God will fulfill His promise.

Your mentoring rests on your trust in Jesus. Trust Him to lead you to the right people to mentor. Trust that He will provide the wisdom you need to move forward in your relationships with them. The best prayer I have learned to whisper is simply "I trust you, Jesus." I don't know what will happen, or how it will happen, but I know He is in the middle of it. He will direct my path—if I let Him.

These young people are treasures crafted by God Almighty. It's easy to forget that sometimes. Especially when they don't live up to your expectations. Stereotypically, it is harder for this generation to keep commitments, to trust others and to launch into adulthood. They can be self-centered. It's important to remember not all millennials fit the stereotypes. But regardless of a generation's downfalls, they are still made in the image of God and deeply loved by Him. So where do you look for inspiration in mentoring? Look at the beauty grafted into their DNA. You are privileged to reflect back to them the promise you see within them. Do you see how wonderful that is?

God has made each of these wonderful young people with gifts. They are risk-takers that want to change the world. They have the drive, while you have the power of encouragement and experience. It truly is a lovely partnership. The dynamics of a symbiotic relationship: they need you and you need them. They need you to lift them toward their future and you need them to continue the legacy of your church. Oh, Jesus is so good at interweaving our lives with one another!

The Power of Words

As a girl, my family's social life revolved around our church family. Each summer we camped for two weeks with other church families. I remember one summer, the summer between my seventh and eighth grade year, I was running around camp just being a kid. Reverend Chuck Marble stopped me and asked a simple question.

"Do you run track?"

"No," I said, but his follow up stunned me.

"God has given you a gift, don't waste it."

The next year, I ran track. By my sophomore year, I had earned my varsity letter; I was the only of my siblings to accomplish this goal. My senior year I was co-captain—my first leadership opportunity. After college I coached and eventually became the Athletic Director for the school district. All of this because someone encouraged me at age 12 to go out for track and not waste the gift I had been given. It was a small statement that had a great impact.

Your words of encouragement are not wasted; you don't know the impact they will have. Be honest, be intentional, but be liberal with your praise.

But how do you know who to do this for? You can't mentor everyone; the world is too big, and the population too vast to meet the need of everyone we encounter. So how do you know? Good question. The answer? Jesus.

Jesus knows who to match us with. Initially, we are at a loss. Of all the people in the world, how do you know who God has picked for you? You look at a sea of faces and no one stands out. This is the time to pray. Pray first to nurture your fellowship with Jesus. Enjoy His presence. This is how you hear Him. Jesus said in John 10:27 (NLT) "My sheep listen to my voice; I know them, and they follow me." You can't hear Him if you are not in close proximity to Him. This is why we spend time in prayer, study, and worship on a daily basis. Know the voice of Jesus, listen for it, and do what it says.

He may not tell you a specific name. But as you go about your day, you will interact with lots of different people: Be aware. His Holy Spirit, connected to your spirit, will speak to you and you will know. Don't over think this. It is better to reach out and fail than to continue to question and not move. Pray before you interact with others, as you interact with others, and after you interact with others. Don't stop praying (1 Thessalonians 5:17). Psalm 27 tells us to "wait patiently for the Lord. Be brave and courageous. Yes, wait patiently for the Lord" (Psalm 27:14, NLT). Waiting is not stagnant nor passive. It is an active press-forward motion. Ask Him to direct you to those in the crowd who are receptive to what you can offer; then wait for His move.

> Waiting is not stagnant nor passive. It is an active press-forward motion.

With experience, this gets easier. King David yearned for God's direction. Psalm 143:10 says, "Teach me to do your will, for you are my God. May your gracious Spirit lead me forward on a firm footing." Do you hear his heart? We need to pray a similar prayer. We need to ask. Pray with expectation; He answers.

His answers come in various ways. If you are not sure you heard Him, ask yourself the following questions: Who do I already know? Is there a relationship I already have that I could nurture? Who do I see on a regular basis that I don't really know? Make a mental list of the names that come to mind. Continue to pray for these individuals regardless of your contact with them. Be alert to His direction and He will show you; be patient as you wait for the next step.

Remember—God promises to lead you. Your job is to follow his lead, not question if He will. Second Corinthians 2:14 promises "But thank God! He has made us his captives and continues to lead us along in Christ's triumphal procession. Now he uses us to spread the knowledge of Christ everywhere, like a sweet perfume."

You're allowed to misunderstand Him, but instead of a mistake, look at it more as a misstep. If you ask Him to lead He will redirect any missteps—and missteps are better than inaction. Some never start because they fear imperfection. But God doesn't demand perfection. He uses willing servants—trust Him with your service. I have asked numerous young women and nothing developed. It is okay; it is not personal. It does not define who you are. Take the risk and ask.

Be willing. You don't have to know where you're going or who He is sending your way. Have a heart like Isaiah: "Here I am, send me" (Isaiah 6:8 NLT). *The surrendered spirit is the one God will use. It is not if He can—it is when He will.*

It's not always easy, however. Building relationships takes determination and vision. Purpose to invite new people. I know Sunday morning is busy—you can't possibly talk to everyone. You must choose to build new bridges. Take time to greet someone you've never talked to before. The younger generation is waiting to be approached by you. Ignoring them, thinking they are not interested in you, has the opposite effect. They interpret it as you don't see them and you don't care to know them. Are they invisible to you? My guess is no—otherwise you would not be investing time in this study. Simply saying hello begins the process. (More on that later!)

The Command to Mentor

The book of Judges warns against deserting the next generation: they will abandon the Lord (See Judges 2). As a mentor, it is your job to partner with them and encourage them into leadership within the church. Encourage their relationship with God and with other believers. The more they incorporate themselves within the body of Christ, the stronger they will become. In turn, they can be both a fruitful member of the Church at large as well as in their community.

They will influence those around them, drawing others to a life in Christ.

But mentoring is about more than staving off death. It's not about resuscitating the church, but tapping into the promise of the future. Stand on those who came before you as you now hoist up the next generation in hope. Jesus is alive in them. His Holy Spirit burns inside. Your job is to fan the flame.

> The younger generation is not just the future church, they are the church NOW.

Can you imagine if every person you know took this call seriously? A huge number of people would be reached at multiple levels of faith. Your combined actions could produce a whole lot of heat that would bring warmth, restoration, and passion to the Church. Remember the younger generation is not just the future church, they are the church NOW.

Mentoring will fortify your local church, but it goes beyond just filling pews on Sunday morning. This is about the transformation of two generations: the older generation must rise to the challenge of the great commission (Matthew 28:16-20), and the next is to become devoted followers of Christ. You carry on an old tradition that is still relevant today. You need to speak in ways they understand without compromising the truth. It's a delicate balance but you can do it. The first step is to initiate so that you, too may see the words of Jeremiah alive and well in your life. Reach out, befriend, and nurture your hope and future. Build your legacy.

Lord: You see the one reading these words. Captivate their heart, give them courage to risk. Help them find the young person you want them to encourage. Help us to see your Spirit in the next generation. Thank you Lord, that you are our hope and future. Thank you that we your church will live on in the next generation. In Jesus Name, AMEN.

Questions:

1. How are you actively pressing forward in your pursuit of God's plan for you?

2. Has God give you a person to pursue? Write their name her. If not—keep asking.

3. How can you initiate the removal of the generational wall in your community?

4. Prayerfully prepare and ask God. Who are you to befriend? Be open to the possibilities—He may surprise you. He orders your world—if you let Him. I promise it is a delightful ride that brings unexpected joy. Are you ready to take this journey?

Chapter Eight: Bridge the Gap – The importance of Unity.

She's twenty-something. By law, she's an adult. Decisions bombard her daily that could affect the rest of her life. One day she is bold, the next she is intimidated. She wants a mentor. Someone she trusts. Someone she knows to be real—you know, authentic. Not just a blind match but someone who knows her. But no one seems to fit her criteria.

Another woman, sitting in the same room, listening to the same sermon, sits four rows back.

She is older. Her children are older. She wants to mentor. Why doesn't someone organize a mentoring group? she thinks. That was the way, she knew, it had always been done. They were matched and got to know each other. The younger women listened to the older women, and they learned how to be godly women, to be women of impact. She wondered why they didn't do that anymore.

But here's the thing. The younger woman doesn't want to be matched with a random stranger. How can she trust just anyone? The older woman seems to care for others but she ignores younger.

I'll just wait, thinks the younger woman.

The older woman noticed the younger woman looked her way after the service. Next time she sees her she'll smile. Next time she will say hello.

Next time, she thinks. But not today. She'll just wait.

This scenario is played out weekly in churches across America. Here we sit on either side of the generation gap, each one waiting for the other one to move. But time is of the essence; younger people leave the church everyday. The disunity between the generations crumbles millennials from within. Some of these millennials are the only Christians in their family; they don't know how to love Jesus, or be like Him, without people like you. Your life can be a personal impact zone for the Kingdom of God.

> Your life can be a personal impact zone for the Kingdom of God.

Not long ago, I sat with a group of twenty-somethings and asked what they wanted from the older women in their church. They said things like:

"I want to be noticed. Say hello. Don't walk by like I'm invisible."

"Someone who has shared experiences with me. Someone who became a Christian as an adult."

"Someone who has experienced similar pain. Someone who is the only Christian in their family."

You know what I noticed? Not one young woman asked for a person of knowledge, highly educated in the things of God or learned in her field. There was not one request for perfection; only common ground.

Your job, dear reader, is to find one person (or more!) and build common ground.

Actively seek out your "Timothy"; aim for the Paul-Timothy relationship described in the opening of 1 Timothy—"Paul, an apostle of Christ Jesus by the command of God our Savior and of Christ Jesus our hope, to Timothy my true son in the faith: Grace, mercy and peace from God the Father and Christ Jesus our Lord" (I Timothy 1:1-2 NIV). Get involved. Chase down your Timothy and start building.

Don't Give Up

But when you don't get involved in mentoring—when you give up—your passivity produces division. Division happens when you're not working with Jesus. And, if you aren't working with Jesus, you are working against Him. That sounds like quite an indictment, but division only needs a small crack to make a gaping hole. And

> Has our busyness caused a misalignment with Jesus?

that hole pushes the generation gap even farther apart. Your inactivity, then, does not encourage any mending of this hole. It does not bridge the chasm. It does not encourage fellowship.

Perhaps, if I may be so bold, your inactivity within the church is caused by your over activity outside of church.

I got a text from a young friend the other day asking this question: "Why can't I develop community at my church?" There are many reasons, but I think one of the biggest is because we are too busy, and we have pushed community to a place of non-priority. It gets lost in our hectic schedules, and I honestly believe we have forgotten how to connect. Has our busyness caused a misalignment with Jesus?

Jesus talked about our need for connection and interaction. The New Testament people lived in an agricultural society, dependent on the crops they produced for survival. They related to descriptive parables Jesus used based on the fruits they grew, but the parables' impact is still powerful today, too.

> We are to love grandly, empowered by His sacrificial love.

Jesus tells us He is the vine and we are the branches (John 15). There is no illness in the vine because Jesus is the perfect source for growth. He is not weak, He can support as many branches that want to be part of his vine. The problem with withering fruit is with us, the branches. The branches need to support each other—when we don't have the support we need we can start to wander, even grow wild and lose our way. Fruit never fully develops. And, if the branch is young and tender, it can be easily broken off.

John 15 reminds us the pruning of branches is necessary. However, it must be done by THE Gardener: God the Father. Not us. We should not try to prune one another! We can guide, yes, but our guidance must point to God, not ourselves. And all we share must be shared in love and grace.

The younger generation—millennials, right now—need the guidance and support you can give. They need to know they matter. They need to know someone sees them. Otherwise they will drift away and stop attending church since they feel they don't matter to anyone. They will leave your community and maybe no one will notice. So it's up to you; will you let them wither and fall away?

In John 15, Jesus continues the discussion on connection, and exhorts believers to give their all for others. "This is my commandment: Love each other in the same way I have loved you. There is no greater love than to lay down one's life for one's friends" (John 15:12-13 NLT).

But here's the thing: Jesus didn't suggest love—He commanded it. But, remember, He does not tell us to do anything he hasn't done himself or provided the means for us to do. We are to love grandly, empowered by His sacrificial love. Oh, Jesus, thank you for equipping us for this great calling to love your people.

So yes, clearly, support and connection is important. But how? How exactly do you connect in order to undergird—to support—one another? You must bridge the gap, step out of your comfort zone, and extend yourself to the next generation. Building bridges is no easy feat, and it requires a plan.

Building Bridges

The "generation gap" became a popular term in the 1960s, and happens generation after generation. As adolescents enter adulthood, they recognize that those that came before them were flawed. Young and idealistic, they forge ahead, determined to make the world a better place. Often this means a rebellion against, or at least challenging the status quo.

Sometimes this accomplishes great things—my generation facilitated great move in technology. We went from renting VCRs with our videos to movies on-demand in a mere thirty year timespan. Today's tech-savvy teens have far surpassed our abilities in this fairly new industry, and I still struggle to relate to their preference of Netflix over cable TV.

But here's an interesting observation amid the technology craze: Millennials still desire connection—it just looks a little different. For example, they desire constant contact via smart phones—texting and social media. But, plugged in, they step out of community living. In a crowd, their phone is a safe place to hide and avoid making eye contact, hoping they won't have an awkward conversation. Technology is a wonderful tool that can lead to isolation. But as the older generation, perhaps less fluent in the language of technology, we still need to understand this world and enter in. Engage.

As women, we still have a deep need for connection. We thrive in safe relationships with other women. We have tendency however, to congregate with others in the same life stage. We look for those who have common interests and share common life events. We don't venture out of that group, and we miss profound opportunities by doing so. Each generation can learn from each other. The older generation has life experience and wisdom to share. The younger generation can challenge us to look at the world in a new way. Their energy inspires us to adventure, and take risks. As I approach the empty nest it is tempting to settle into a life of ease. But that is not what God calls us to do. We are to live a life that gives. Every generation has much to give to each other.

Older women must understand the perspective of younger women. If you were 20 years old, how would you face the challenges of today's world? For me, I know just the pressure of social media would do me in. I'm sure I would post all sorts of embarrassing tidbits. Today's twenty-somethings have high expectations for their life. They are labeled the entitlement generation. Stereotypically, my generation knew we had to work to earn our way in life; millennials feel it is owed them. Of course we need to be careful when we make blanket statements, but it is a subtle, yet comment social phenomenon for this generation. They see the fulfillment of their dreams as a right instead of an earned privilege. They expect us to know that and reward them for their willingness instead of proof of the hard work.

There are significant circumstances that have led to the entitlement phenomenon. Exposure of untrustworthy leaders, child-centered homes, and participation rewards are the cultural choices that have brought us to this societal battle. In our attempt to build safe environments and nurture strong self-esteems, we created a narcissistic generation. However, I believe this is a teachable generation, IF we work to understand them. As mentors, our awareness of this phenomenon is key. We need to look at the why in order to understand how deal with the reality of the situation.

National Distrust

My children's childhood was overshadowed by national embarrassment. Sex scandals in the government and the church shaped their environment. Even if our children were sheltered from the news, my generation was changed by these events. We didn't hesitate to talk negatively around the dinner table about those that had fallen from grace, and it infiltrated the TV shows we watched. Sarcastic and caustic comments describing leaders are the norm. Distrust of authority is now common place. In the process, we no longer revere these positions; we are wary of them. Respect is not given automatically; it is earned.

National distrust is now prevalent in schools and the workplace. Teachers fight to prove themselves. A boss is not esteemed until deemed worthy of the honor. It is a turn from our parents' generation; I was only seven years old when President Nixon resigned. I can tell you exactly where I was as I listened with my parents. It was a historical moment for us. It was the first person in authority in my life that failed me. It isn't your responsibility to dissuade millennials from this idea. Understand it—insight and understanding makes you a better mentor. You build trust by your respectful behavior, increasing loyalty and opportunity to speak into their lives.

Because of this inherent lack of trust, you may find millennials do not respond to your initial interaction. They may sit back and observe you. Are you worth their respect? I know this sounds harsh, but they are self-protective. And guess what? We are the ones who taught them that. Patience and honesty will overcome their reluctance. It is not a personal affront; it is a generational behavior. While outright disrespect should be corrected, it is a challenge you must meet with grace.

Helicopter Parenting

In addition to modeling disrespect to authority figures, we sheltered our children. September 11th forever changed our country. It exposed our vulnerability to foreign attacks. A new enemy was at our doorstep and we were woefully unprepared for their unique warfare. I sat stunned, revolted by the reality of the violent world we live in as the day's events unfolded. My children were young, and that day our parenting as a nation changed. Suddenly, my safe world dissolved around me, and grief swept over me. Deep in my soul I feared for my children's future. Already child-centric, we became even more protective. This one event changed our outlook. We became more protective. We recognized life is fragile in a new way. We tried to bubble wrap their world.

Despite our efforts, the Millennial Generation has grown up under the shadow of violence. Afghanistan, Iraq, Columbine, and Virginia Tech—locations that immediately relate to carnage—all occurred in their lifetime. A tired reality, they fight back with love and service. We showed we cared by drawing others into the protective environment of our church. Now they are taking the church to those in need. This is a beautiful response to an ugly world. Encourage this kind of risk. Their risk is Jesus-centered, and we can learn from it.

In addition, we showered our children with awards. Our intentions were noble—after all, no one wants to feel like a loser. Policies were started to award kids just for their participation. Every child received a trophy, no matter what they accomplished. They learned to expect a snack at half-time and an award at the end of the season. In one sense, there is nothing wrong with this. But it becomes a problem when those that go above and beyond aren't recognized. The message sent precipitates a lazy attitude: why should I work so hard, if everyone will win in the end?

Now, these children are adults. You've heard all the generalizations and stereotypes. Their generation struggles to launch into independent lives; our generation struggles with helicopter parenting. Their generation is narcissistic; our generation enables them. They take greater risks, but only because they expect us to be their safety net. They question belief systems, but don't really know how to live out their newly-defined world view.

Somewhere along the way, we forgot to teach the beauty of hard work. Lofty goals should be encouraged but if they aren't willing to work for them, they will not be attained. We have told them they are destined for greatness but forgot to explain it won't

> Each breath is a gift; our days are numbered.

just happen without hard work. Mundane days are a necessary part of creating something impactful. This teaches perseverance. Romans reminds us that this "endurance develops strength of character, and character strengthens our confident hope of salvation" (Romans 5:4 NLT). We must set the example, and live in the moment. Each breath is a gift; our days are numbered. Don't waste the mundane days wishing for something more. Count them as beautiful. This example will encourage and teach the next generation to do the same.

We forgot to teach Ecclesiastes: "Yet God has made everything beautiful for its own time. He has planted eternity in the human heart, but even so, people cannot see the whole scope of God's work from beginning to end" (Ecclesiastes 3:11 NLT). Life is a process and it's in the process that we grow. Contentment without complacency is a difficult goal but it is possible.

While encouraging the high expectations, we should also remind them they have more to learn. This is true for all of us! Never stop learning. This has to be self-recognized. Our job is to be aware of ourselves and also guide them in their pursuit of adulthood. Strong opinions fly from their mouths. Their bravado is a protective layer designed to keep the world out. Only the trustworthy are allowed beyond it. Patience with one another is key; humility speaks volumes to them. I don't mean to step on your toes. But it's something to think about.

Jesus is the Center

Unfortunately, our society encourages isolation. We don't sit on our front porches and shoot the breeze with our neighbors anymore. After church, most people hurry home to get on with their day. You have to purpose and intentionally connect with each another.

Jesus expects us to be in unity, actually. But we are the ones who cause disunity and division. Ignoring and even rejecting one another is like rejecting Him. OUCH!! Jesus didn't tell us to become one. He said we ARE one, just like He is one with the Father. (See John 17:11.) is not His prayer request for us to stay together; it is His declaration of our existing unity. Nurture this unity.

Why? Unity and God's glory. Others will believe and know God's love as they witness our unity and love for each other (John 17:21-24)!

Oh how I love this chapter in Scripture. It is entirely Jesus' words. Think about that—a King, praying for us. THE KING, praying for us! WHAT?!? Yes! This chapter is incredibly personal, powerful, persuasive. It is the declaration of who we are in Him—brothers and sisters in Christ. Members of the Kingdom, ambassadors with the call of grace. John 17 is the pronouncement of His expectations— a high order but He will empower us. Take time to read this chapter, and read it from a mentor prospective.

Jesus prays for our holiness. Remember—holiness does not mean perfection. Ironically, in a discussion of unity, holiness means to separate oneself. However, it's not a separation from people but from sin. Your life should look different. You are set apart to do God's work. As a mentor, learn God's truth—which will make you holy—and live by it (John 17:17).

As you live this kind of life, He grows in you. In John 17:26, Jesus says, "I have revealed you to them, and I will continue to do so. Then your love for me will be in them, and I will be in them" (NLT). With this we have God's love in you. This is how you are empowered to love the next generation. This is how you unified with God and with one another.

This process is really quite simple to start; you may be doing this already and not even aware. If you want to bridge the gap, don't wait for them to come to you. Be bold and greet someone new from a different generation. Throughout the New Testament the church is encouraged to greet one another in love—to build the church on love. This is why Paul wrote "here is my greeting in my own handwriting" (I Corinthians 16:21 NLT); He wanted to make it personal.

Be realistic, though. Don't expect to be instant friends. Building bridges takes time and thoughtful engineering. First Corinthians 3:10-11 says, "Because of God's grace to me, I have laid the foundation like an expert builder. Now others are building on it.

> Combine your experience and wisdom with their passion and energy, and you'll change the world.

But whoever is building on this foundation must be very careful. For no one can lay any foundation other than the one we already have—Jesus Christ." Here, Paul was referring to the preaching of Jesus

Christ in Corinth, not necessarily building relationships, but his metaphor can be powerfully applied. Jesus is your foundation, and then from there you can continue building. Jesus is the center of your budding friendship.

Linking Arms

Following Jesus' directive of unity will link the generations together. Just imagine what can be accomplished when we work together. "How good and pleasant it is when God's people live together in unity" (Psalm 133:1, NIV). Combine your experience and wisdom with their passion and energy, and you'll change the world. It can happen, one relationship at a time.

Do you see the promise here? Do you see the potential? Lay down your apprehension and move forward. Do what you can to build a bridge. Your bridge will interconnect with other bridges to create a network.

A caution in your initial outreach: be careful not to judge. It will destroy all the work you've done to build your bridge. Understand the culture—their sarcasm and biting comments are society-driven and not necessarily from a hardened heart. It is a reflection of their wit, not their spiritual growth. However, you do not have to play their game. Oh, I love to be funny! And I love to appear as intelligent, but my comments will never bite back. We must be a classy example not a poor imitation.

One day on a whim, my daughter and I watched cartoons together. What an eye opener to today's culture! Instead of a nostalgic throwback, we were a bit shocked. The characters were catty with each other; children's shows have been infected by the mean girl culture, and it's being portrayed as witty and sophisticated. Yet it can tear at the fibers of the heart, hardening the user and wounding the receiver. And this is "normal" for the younger generation!

Today, girls learn women are sarcastic, and quick with comebacks that sting. Women are tough, they don't take it personally. Sassy is attractive. Respect is no longer important. Teasing is all part of the game.

And my generation responds by clucking our tongues in disapproval, driving further the wedge between us.

This is a confusing time to be an adolescent. Societies' foundation is rocky; if young women are rooted just in society, they have little direction and even less security. We need to be a safe place for them. Demonstrate kindness. Even our correction is to be rooted in love.

My friend and her husband own a business. Most of their employees are millennial young men. She was frustrated with them because their actions and choices didn't make sense. One young man complained a great deal—so much that his boss referred to him as "the whiner." Recently, the young man approached his bosses. "I have some concerns. Can we talk?" Remembering the millennial generation's need to be heard, they sat down and listened. They respected his feelings but could do little to change the work situation as it was their busy season. Yet, after the fact, he complained less, all because they listened! The moral of the story is—give your young friend a voice. You will be amazed at what it does for their confidence and attitude.

BUT. Don't tell them what to do. Pushy people intimidate and anger twenty-somethings. They probably won't tell you that; they'll just walk away and avoid you in the future. Treat them as a peer. Respect goes a long way. I recently saw a post on Tumblr, a social media website, that said, "You are not obligated to respect adults that do not respect you." While this is perhaps not the best advice for Millennials entering the workforce, this is indeed the voice of this generation.

It is the responsibility of your generation to understand the next generation. Accept them without enabling them. Let them fail without rescuing. Coach when advice is requested without directing every step. Their generation is creative, inspired, and energetic. Partnering together, you can change the world and build a legacy.

Recently, I partnered with Annie (age 25) on a Sole Hope Shoe Cutting Party (www.solehope.org), where we get a group of women together to cut material for the soles of shoes to be sent to a different country. We gathered materials and invited friends. We made a great team, because I have experience promoting these kind of events, and Annie did mission work in Uganda the past two summers and will return this summer. Together we were motivated to make this a successful event. The night of the party I looked around the room. I realized the ages of the women ranged from 19 to 60—that is a successful intergenerational event! It was not our goal, but it happened because we partnered together. In the end we cut 80 pairs of shoe tops that will be made to protect children against jigger infection.

Relationships like these have the potential to be an extraordinary example to our community. When others see the strength of the connections formed, they will be curious. Is this real? Has it been tested? There are powerful long term effects of reaching out! They will look closer to see what you have—because you are different. You are set apart. You are united. Your goal is show them Jesus. At the center of each of these relationships, He reigns.

"For your kingdom is an everlasting kingdom. You rule throughout all generations. The Lord always keeps his promises; he is gracious in all he does" (Psalm 145:13 NLT). You are a reflection of His promise and His grace. Choose to shine on the next generation in unity and build His church.

Father. I lift up those that are reading this. May they understand hear You and Your encouragement to be the person You created them to be. I pray that we each reach out to support one another. That we love unabashedly your people. In Jesus Name, AMEN

Questions:

1. Did you initiate a contact after the last chapter? Describe your experience.

2. What insight did you gain from the description of millennials?

3. How can you build a bridge? What action can you do?

Chapter Nine—Building Trust

Pain washed across Caitlin's face as she approached me. My mother instincts took over, and I asked what the problem was. She's diabetic, and the lead to her insulin pump had been slammed in the trunk of a car, ripping it from her skin. My stomach flip-flopped at her description. Fiercely independent, she had long ago learned to take care of herself. She assured me that no, she didn't need a doctor, yes it hurt, and yes, she knew what to do. It seemed like a big deal to me but not to her. Our conversation ended, and crisis averted.

Soon I forgot about the whole thing but she didn't. A few moments of kindness impressed her, and it was the beginning of a friendship. You never know what God will use.

When I saw her on Sundays, I'd great her each time, but honestly, I was not being intentional. I had now idea she was paying attention. Needless to say, I've learned the importance of a simple hello. Respecting others enough to acknowledge them goes a long way. Paul gives this instruction to Timothy, particularly regarding his interaction with women. "Treat older women as you would your mother, and treat younger women with all purity as you would your own sisters" (1 Timothy 5:2 NLT).

Building trust begins here.

Faithful in the Little Things

> Living a transparent life speaks volumes to this generation.

It's true we're imperfect, and we will never be perfect. But living a consistent life of integrity isn't the same as perfection. Acknowledging our mistakes, asking forgiveness, living with integrity and consistency can be so impactful. Living a transparent life speaks volumes to this generation.

Yes, it's had and it takes determination. It's easy to rationalize our errors and indiscretions, but the next generation sees it all, and knows more than you think about our generation. Our justification looks like hypocrisy to them. Hypocrites. Actors. People who pretend to be someone else. And—untrustworthy.

Living a consistent life of integrity is impactful. This isn't the same as perfection, so don't feel the pressure to be perfect. You will make mistakes, but acknowledge them and ask forgiveness if needed. Live a transparent life—it speaks volumes to this generation. Yes, it's hard and it takes determination. It's easy to rationalize away errors. But the younger generation is watching and knows more than you think about our generation. Justification looks like hypocrisy to them.

Hypocrites. Actors. People who pretend to be someone else. And—to them—untrustworthy.

This is not a new problem. It dates as far back as ancient Israel. King David had a large family and Scripture paints a not-so-pretty picture of his parenting. He seemed to be somewhat inattentive. Second Samuel 13 describes David's son Amnon sexually abusing his half-sister, Tamar. While Tamar, shamed, went to live in isolation with her brother Absolam, David left Amnon's sin unpunished. Two years later, after David had done nothing, Absolam took action and killed Amnon. Needless to say, life got messier for David's family after that and not to mention for the Kingdom, too.

So let's use King David and Absolam in a little analogy here. King David represents us (the older generation) and Absolam represents the next generation. If we do not take action, we are ineffective leaders, and the next generation will act if we don't. Their actions—like Absolam's—may be rash, but from their point of view, they are just. But they may not examine the consequences ahead of time.

However, this isn't always a bad attribute to have. Even If we aren't actively, effectively pursuing Jesus, they will without us. And like Absolam, they are passionate. Can't blame them for that!

On the other hand, it can be quite an indictment for us. Remember that verse in Luke that says, "if you are faithful in little things, you will be faithful in large ones. But if you are dishonest in little things, you won't be honest with greater responsibilities" (Luke 16:10)? Yeah—twentysomethings live by this verse. They watch for consistency and faithfulness in the little things. They look at your relationships, your ministry, your work ethic, your family—everything. They notice the little things. So, no pressure.

Faithfulness implies commitment. Long term repetition of consistent behavior. Luke 16:10 is specifically referring to wealth, but Jesus makes sure we understand our ability with money reflects our ability to handle all gifts responsibly. The "little" refers to size, amount, and humility. Do you consistently care about the little things as well as the big? Or are you too dignified to do the smaller inelegant acts of service? And are you the same behind closed doors as you are in public?

This returns us to the earlier question of authenticity, another trait highly valued by the younger generation. Are you consistently authentic—are you authentic the time? (If you're not, then you're not really authentic, are you?) Authentic people are trustworthy, honest, faithful servants who don't expect a reward. They're reliable without supervision, consistent in service, and don't complain or grumble. Doing things simply because it's the right thing to do quietly builds the reputation of a reliable servant—a trustworthy, authentic leader.

Jesus demonstrated this throughout his ministry. He was willing to do the great miracles but he didn't ignore the daily acts of service. He welcomed little children. He had time for the widows. He washed the disciples' feet, and instructed us to follow his example (John 13:15). I love that he was so clear with his instructions—the difference between a servant heart and task master; He is not demanding anything of us that He did not do Himself.

So...are you willing to follow His example?

Caitlin, the young diabetic woman I described at the beginning of the chapter, lived with us for short time. The house she grew up in was different from ours. She was surprised by the quiet in our home. Certainly we had disagreements, frustrations, and our share of grumpiness. However, it was the way we handled those moments that impressed her. Again, we are not perfect but we try to use Biblical standards in conflict. It is a rarity for our voices to be raised. My purpose in telling you this is we chose to live this way. We implemented what we were taught as best we could. My husband and I examined our own natural tendencies. We agreed to work on our weaknesses. We also agreed to give each other grace when we screwed up. Mistakes happen, and in our house we strive to be quick to forgive. This does not mean conflicts are ignored, it means we deal with them in a respectful manner.

Just do IT!

I am not a brave person. I like to talk but I don't like to make phone calls. Scheduling appointments freak me out; even if it is for a haircut or doctor appointment. I know that doesn't make sense. It overwhelms me to call and figure out a date, especially if it is for one of my kids. Coordination of all that information feels like more than I can handle. This shouldn't be hard—after all, when I contact a business it benefits them as well as me. Yet, it is still hard. I put it off. Whatever the reason, I need to get over it and do what I have to do. The same is true for you. Get over the apprehension and just do it.

I know, that sounds trite and insensitive, doesn't it? "Get over it and just do it!" But, to be honest, it really is that simple. It might not be easy but it is simple. And It is definitely going to be worth it.

But how do you know who to do this for? You can't mentor everyone; the world is too big, and the population too vast to meet the need of everyone we encounter. So how do you know? Good question. The answer? I don't have it. But Jesus does!

> You can't hear Him if you are not close to Him—don't roam out of earshot from Him.

Jesus knows who to match you with. Initially, you may be at a loss. Of all the people in the world, how do you know who God has picked for you? You look at a sea of faces and no one stands out. This is the time to pray. Pray first to nurture your fellowship with Jesus. Enjoy His presence. This is how you hear Him. Jesus said "My sheep listen to my voice; I know them, and they follow me" (John 10:27 NLT). You can't hear Him if you are not close to Him—don't roam out of earshot from Him. Stay close by spending time in prayer, study, and worship on a daily basis. Know the voice of Jesus, listen for it, and do what it says.

Jesus may not give you a specific name. But as you go about your day, you will interact with lots of different people: be aware. His Holy Spirit, connected to your spirit, will speak to you and you will know. Don't overthink this. It is better to reach out and fail than to continue to question and not move. Pray before you interact with others, as you interact with others, and after you interact with others. Don't stop praying (1 Thessalonians 5:17). Psalm 27 tells us to wait. "Wait patiently for the Lord. Be brave and courageous. Yes, wait patiently for the Lord" (Psalm 27:14 NLT). Waiting is not stagnant nor passive. It is an active press-forward motion. Ask Him to direct you to those in the crowd who are receptive to what you can offer; then wait for His move.

With experience, this gets easier. King David yearned for God's direction. He wrote, "Teach me to do your will, for you are my God. May your gracious Spirit lead me forward on a firm footing" (Psalm 143:10 NLT) Do you hear his heart? We need to pray a similar prayer. We need to ask. Pray with expectation; He answers.

His answers come in various ways. These questions can help you look around and see who might be a good fit: Who do I already know? Is there a relationship I already have that I could nurture? Who do I see on a regular basis that I don't really know? Make a mental list of the people that come to mind. Continue to pray for these individuals regardless of your contact with them. Be alert to His direction and He will show you; be patient as you wait for the next step.

> But God doesn't demand perfection. He uses willing servants—trust Him with your service.

Remember—God promises to lead you. Your job is to follow His lead, not question if He will. You're allowed to misunderstand Him, but instead of a mistake, look at it more as a misstep. If you ask Him to lead He will redirect any missteps. This is better than inaction. Some never start because they fear imperfection. But God doesn't demand perfection. He uses willing servants—trust Him with your service. I have asked numerous young women and nothing developed. It is okay; it is not personal. It does not define who you are. Take the risk and ask.

Be willing. You don't have to know where you're going or who He is sending your way. Have a heart like Isaiah: "Here I am. Send me" (Isaiah 6:8). The surrendered spirit is the one God will use. It is not if He can—it is when He will.

Initiate: Be Bold!

It's not always easy, I know. Building relationships takes determination and vision. Have a plan and stick to it. Purpose to invite new people. I know Sunday morning is busy—you can't possibly talk to everyone. But you must choose to initiate with just one. Be bold and greet someone new from a different generation.

Throughout the New Testament the church is encouraged to greet one another in love—to build the church on love. We must continue to build the church on love. The younger generation is waiting to be approached by you. Ignoring them, thinking they are not interested in you has the opposite effect. They interpret it as you don't see them and you don't care to know them. Are they invisible to you? My guess is no—otherwise you would not have picked up this book.

Simple actions make a huge difference. Greeting them and calling someone by name communicates their importance. They are craving to be recognized. Lacking trust, they avoid the first move, while fear of rejection shuts your mouth. Be the one to step out and risk.

When you see a younger person, smile and look them in the eyes. Most of the time they will smile back. Take a moment, say hi and ask their name. Remember their name and use it the next time you see them. Do you have a bad memory? Write it down. Tell them you are old and can't remember, make a joke of it. A personal touch like this speaks volumes. This is so simple, yet so powerful. It communicates they're important and valuable.

Recently, my daughter was greeted by the head director of the Theater Department at her college. "Mom, she knew my nickname! She called me by my nickname!" It communicated familiarity; my daughter was no longer a face in the crowd. This is also done throughout Scripture, when the writers of the letters greet others by name. Follow their example. Paul demonstrated this in Romans: "Give my greetings to Priscilla and Aquila, my co-workers in the ministry of Christ Jesus" (Romans 16:3 NLT).

As your comfort level increases, invite them to spend time with you. Keep in mind each of these steps are a form of an invitation. Your job is to invite and keep that invitation open. Jesus encouraged this: "For I was hungry and you gave me something to eat, I was thirsty and you gave me something to drink, I was a stranger and you invited me in" (Matthew 25:35 NIV). The next generation is the church of today, not just the future church. Treat them as such.

Be creative. This is not hard but it must be deliberate. "So then, let us aim for harmony in the church and try to build each other up" (Romans 14:19 NLT).

Amber always enthusiastically greeted me. Her bubbly personality is infectious. After a few months, however, her friend, Mary, asked me why I never greeted her in that manner. It started as a joke. The next time I saw Mary, I squealed and yelled her name. After that, each time she saw me she did the same thing. It was silly and undignified and it drew more attention than I really wanted—though I will admit it's not completely out of my extroverted character. But it became our thing. It broke the generation barrier between Mary and me. We don't do that anymore, but there is still a bond, a mutual respect that started with a squeal and a joke. Thanks, Mary, for teaching me to be silly!

Be realistic, though. Don't expect to be instant friends. It takes time. Jesus is your foundation, and then from there you can continue building. You cannot force mentoring, especially with the millennial generation, but they will always appreciate the friendship, whether or not it becomes mentoring or discipling. They have uncertainty in their lives about inadequacies whether social, academic, or physical. They will not begin the conversation for fear of rejection, but need—and want—you to initiate the process. Make the first move. Start the conversation.

Concentrate on loving that person. The Bible encouraged to love and promises God will no turn a blind eye to your action and service. "For God is not unjust. He will not forget how hard you have worked for him and how you have shown your love to him by caring for other believers, as you still do" (Hebrews 6:10 NLT). Genuine love will break down relationship walls between you and those God has brought

> Genuine love will break down relationship walls between you and those God has brought to you.

to you. Immerse yourself in the Holy Spirit, allowing His fruits to grow in you (Galatians 5)—Imagine the impact you would have if you continually poured out peace, patience, goodness, kindness, love, joy, faithfulness, gentleness, and self-control! It's not an easy task, but nothing is impossible with God (Matthew 19:26)!

The goal is to break down the generational barrier, staying authentic to your character. Don't let the idea of squealing across the room intimidate you. Don't worry—the squeal is not required—though if it fits your personality and hers, it may just do the trick. Take the risk to tear down the generational wall, Squeal or no squeal.

Nurture It!

Make them the center of conversation. Inquire about a specific issue—as long as it's not too personal for the setting you are in. Let them know you are interested in them as a person—the details of their life are important to you. Be specific in your compliments, but make sure they are genuine before they leave your mouth. (Remember, be authentic!)

At first it is fragile. Like any new construction, a relationship or friendship can be unstable until the foundation is firmly in place. Reassure your young mentees they are important, and valuable to you. Each time you reach out it adds another support to your bridge. Soon she will begin to help build this bridge, too. Somewhere on the construction you will meet. And you'll both recognize this structure is one of many that support the Kingdom of God.

Always offer prayer. This is not a social nicety; it is a spiritual discipline. You are volunteering to present your friend's concerns before God Almighty. Take the time to follow through and pray. Ask them how they are doing in this area the next time you see them. Remember your commitment to them and let them know you have not forgotten. You're building trust.

As your friendship grows, they will trust you with information no one else knows. This is an honor you have earned but should be treasured and protected. Keep the information shared confidential. This confidence is a gift only the closest of relationships achieve. Do not take that for granted. When that moment arrives, sit back in awe—the wonder that someone would trust you on such a level is a God thing. His Kingdom grows when we build trustworthy relationships. Hold it close to your heart, guard it, and thank God for it!

Not Your Job To Fix It

As a society, we nurture one another's offenses. We respond to someone's hurt with "you deserve better" or "how dare they!" These may be true statements but we need to make sure our words show empathy. Don't encourage an offense. This is common in women, isn't it? We encourage others to right the wrong and justify condemnation when we need to move them toward forgiveness and love. When it happens to you, be the example.

I don't like it when others hurt, but it's not always my responsibility to fix it—just to care. Investing in others means risking one-sided love. Rarely does that occur but it is possible. If you seek a relationship to meet your needs, look somewhere else. This one has to be about the younger friend. That being said, you will receive benefits you didn't know would come. Once trust is earned, loyalty will be yours. In general, this generation does not give trust easily but once earned they will be loyal for life.

Respect Boundaries

Further develop communication with those God has encouraged you to pursue. Go where they are—like social media—but be yourself. Social media can be a safe place to build structure in your relationship. You can learn about what is important to them by their status updates, photos, videos, and articles they post. Commenting and remembering detail communicates they are important to you.

Use proper social media etiquette. Your purpose is to develop a relationship not to be a creeper. If they post something of sensitive nature, discuss it privately by private message or in person. Be discerning, nothing will stop a relationship faster than embarrassing them online. Remember anyone can read what is posted in social networks. Do not use this venue to give unsolicited advice.

Always respect their boundaries. You are communicating your availability, but accept that not all are interested in befriending you. Everyone, however, benefits from hospitality. You may never move past this point in the relationship. That is okay. In ministry you need tough skin but a soft heart.

That being said, there is no formula to build these relationships. I meet many young people one on one. Going for coffee is a great way to have a discussion. (More on that later!) This however may not happen right away. Invest time in neutral places. Greet them at church events, invite them to sit with you at a service, inquire about work or school. Like any investment, though, it needs time. Trust must grow, because without trust, you have no relationship. Invest your faithfulness to grow their trust.

Listen

I would much rather tell people my opinion than listen to theirs. If you're an extrovert, you probably just nodded your head. But remind yourself why you meet together. Learn to listen. All your advice will fall on deaf ears if you're not willing to listen. This is not time to teach lessons or quote Scripture. Listen to what is said, reflect it back, and listen some more. They don't always want to hear what you think they should do. Wait to be asked.

Not only are we quiet during our time together but afterwards as well. The conversation you shared is to remain confidential. The only time you may need to break confidence is if what they share with you puts them or someone else in danger. But as a general rule, never, ever discuss the content with anyone, especially their family. They need a safe place. My kids each have confided in other adults. I don't know what is shared. If it is important for me to know eventually it will come to me. I know that may seem counter intuitive but it helps them build autonomy. This is what we want! Independent productive adults who work to build God's Kingdom.

> Need more fruit? Give God more time.

Accept the Challenge Is all this idealistic? Probably. That has always been a problem for me. But think of it more as a challenge.

Don't sell yourself short. Don't give up before you try. Remember, the fruits of the Spirit are the direct result of spending time with the Lord. They are not earned or learned. They become infused in us because of our relationship with him. Need more fruit? Give God more time. Welcome Him into all you do. Do not compartmentalize your relationship with Jesus. If you do the fruits will stay in those boxes, too. Let Him in; I'm telling you—it will blow up your spiritual walk—in a good way.

That is one of the beautiful parts of this journey. I didn't start with all the tools I needed. As I moved through these relationships, I have learned so much. My purpose is to give, yet I get so much in return. And I have become a better person.

Stay malleable. Allow God to continue to form you. No matter how old you get, you can continue to grow. Now that is a delightful thought! The Lord is always crafting you. You were created in your mother's womb, but God continues to work on you. You are His workmanship, His masterpiece.

Thank you Lord that you are not done with me!

As a mentor, prayer is essential. Failure to pray leads to failure in mentoring. Circumstances you face together may overwhelm both of you. You have a constant life line, but a lifeline does you no good if you don't reach for it. You must reach out to the Lord on a consistent basis. Matthew 6:3 teaches to seek the Kingdom first and live a righteous life. If you think

> You were created in your mother's womb, but God continues to work on you. You are His workmanship, His masterpiece.

about it too long, that is a tall order. Finding God's Kingdom in the din of today's world is hard. There is a constant pull to look everywhere except at Jesus. Develop the habit of living in Him and in constant communication with Him—this leads to behavior that reflects Him.

Jesus calls you to abide in Him (John 15:4). It is more than an indwelling. You abide in Him when you live in accordance with His ways. Allow Him to be in control; righteousness is a deliberate choice. Make that fresh commitment each morning. Start your day with Him, end your day with Him, and recognize Him throughout your day.

But don't forget to listen, too. I often forget He has something to say! I get so busy dumping my concerns over to Him that I don't stop to hear. He is gentle but He will always speak, and you must have ears to hear Him. Prayer is a conversation—an exchange of information. Tap into His wealth of wisdom daily.

You have to be willing to be honest. Honesty starts with you. Perfection is not possible but improvement can always take place. What areas of your life is God improving? Are you yielding to the Holy Spirit? Trust me, it is only human to commit the same sin over and over. It's a problem, though, when you get comfortable with that sin and accept it. You cannot help others grow in their relationship with Christ if you are not willing to grow yourself. Self-reflection must precede mentoring of others. But don't let self-awareness of your flaws stop you from mentoring. Only let it keep you humble.

As a mentor, you must remain teachable. One benefit you will find is what this generation can teach you. One young woman I meet with ALWAYS asks me how she can pray for me. She supports my ministry through prayer. She listens to my doubts and appreciates my candor. This is a lovely outgrowth of our relationship. After three years of meeting together, we are not just mentoring partners, we are friends. We live life together.

> Surrendered service to Jesus will always bless your life.

Authenticity, humility, honesty, vulnerability, and courage are what attract this generation. I just heard that groan. I know, I know. You are passionate about mentoring but you don't want to open yourself up this way. This, my friend, is something you must learn. A guarded heart cannot grow past the walls you have put into place. Trust Jesus with your hurts and let Him soften the hard places. Remember—"...And we know that in all things God works for the good of those who love him, who have been called according to his purpose" (Romans 8:28 NIV). Jesus will ALWAYS honor that promise, because He works ALL things for our good when you are doing His work.

Surrendered service to Jesus will always bless your life. It is not your motivator, but a result. He will nurture you as you nurture others. Your mentoring relationships are love relationships, and God provides for you as well as works through you to provide for others. (See I John 3:20-23.)

Dear Lord: The initiation of a relationship is hard. I ask that you give each of us direction in this process. Help us to be brave and say hello. Show us how to be tough skinned and soft hearted. Help us to be people of integrity that reflect you. Teach us to be trustworthy in all things. Give us the drive to build your Kingdom. In the Name of Jesus AMEN.

Questions:

1. Define the word "integrity":

2. What are the "little things" you do in your community? How do they add up to build your reputation?

3. Trust and authenticity are closely linked. Describe this relationship:

4. Who is guarding your heart? Is it Jesus or you?

5. What is one area God is improving in you?

6.   Has God given you a person to pursue? Write their name here. If not—keep asking.

Chapter Ten: Letting Go

This is, by far, the most difficult chapter to write—experiencing failure. I'm not ashamed of the failures I'll talk about, but it's still painful. Failure usually is. But pain and failure is as important as success—we learn from both.

> But pain and failure is as important as success—we learn from both.

I know, not the most uplifting way to start a chapter. But stick with me—learn from my mistakes and take comfort for your own.

Let's review mentoring rule number one: mentoring relationships are not about you. True, you will benefit from knowing another of God's children, but hold these dear ones loosely and lovingly; they belong to Jesus.

When You're Just Not Feeling It

Okay, so let's pretend you're new at this. (Because you are, right? Or else you wouldn't be reading this book!) Let's pretend that you have picked someone out. She seems like the perfect match, so you have initiated the relationship, but it feels off. You're not quite sure why, but it does. There is a desire to mentor on your part and a desire to be mentored on their part, but after meeting with her once or twice you just have no chemistry. It's okay—don't give up yet!

It could be that you just aren't a good fit. But give the relationship time—it can feel awkward at first, especially if this is new for you. If after a few months you realize there is a discomfort or even disharmony between you, talk about it. Address it head on; ask her how she feels the relationship is progressing. Come to a mutual agreement—you don't want her to feel rejected. That would be counterproductive.

If she wants to pursue this relationship, take time to examine yourself. Is there anything you could do differently? What is not clicking? Ask questions to get to know her better. Sometimes it is a trust issue, and it takes time to earn her respect and trust. That is okay. Relax, and take the time.

People don't always mesh well; it could be a personality clash. It does not mean you are flawed or inadequate. It simply means it's not the right match. There is nothing wrong with that. Consider offering to help find a better fit.

It might have nothing to do with you at all! Some young women seek a mentoring relationship for the wrong reasons. They are not looking to grow but for confirmation they are making all the right choices. Stuck people are stubborn, and not ready to take responsibility for their own choices. Perhaps they are hoping for ammunition to fire back at those that have wronged them. Obviously, that is not healthy nor is that your intention. The good news is most of these partnerships fizzle out on their own—especially if you are a person of integrity; when they recognize they are not getting what they want, they leave.

This does not mean it is a failure. You always leave an impact even if your interaction is for a short time. Your job is to love them without enabling them. Stand firm—but with gentleness—on God's truth. Don't preach but also don't support wrong choices.

If you work to move the relationship forward and it is to no avail, it is probably time to let go. Leave the mentoring relationship in an amicable way. You can continue to encourage, and when she is ready she may return to you or someone else to be mentored. Keep in mind severing the relationship allows her to learn what a healthy relationship looks like. This is not abandonment—let her know that if you can. But it does teach boundaries for her future relationships.

It is important to remember any relationship is a risk; pain is a possibility. The more you invest in the relationship, the more difficult this becomes. It hurts because you love her and you want God's best for her. If she chooses to reject, it is not your fault.

I have lived this scenario, and I know it's so hard. I still pray for her but I cannot control her. I hate feeling helpless. I want to fix it when they hurt. Yet, fixing it is the last thing they need. What they need is compassion, encouragement, a friend. You cannot fix their problem, but you can remind them they are not alone.

But if their final choice is to reject you as well, then you have to let them go.

> You can guide them there but you cannot do it for them.

You have not failed if your mentee chooses to break off the relationship. Whatever seeds you have planted will always be there. When they are ready, they will turn to the knowledge they gained from you. It may be immediate; it may be years; or sadly, it may be never heeded. But it is not your fault. Love alone cannot fix the broken pieces of another's life; it is the empowerment of the Holy Spirit that makes others whole. You can guide them there but you cannot do it for them.

The Unteachable, The Stuck, The Weighed Down

You also do not want to develop a fruitless relationship; you can meet with and listen to your young friend and see them continue in the same patterns. And it's frustrating when they share their heart but they don't heed your advice. They don't change, and your meetings turn into complaining sessions. It's always everyone else's fault. She is unteachable. This is one that needs heavy prayer: do you address the issue? Do you continue meeting? Do you continue to invest in the relationship?

I have experienced this and it is difficult. She wants to meet but constantly cancels. She asked to be kept accountable but ignores your inquiries. She is only partially honest. She lives her life the way she wants—until there is a crisis. She sits in your kitchen and cries; her life is a disaster. Some of the issues are natural consequences of her own choices, others are just a result of life. Life pours out joys and sorrows on all of us. At times it feels hopeless, and like God is not intervening, and the pain is intense and endless. But no matter what she does, it's not going to get better because it's out of her hands. You must love, and listen but usually you can't fix it. Her pain is your pain, and the burden is heavy. But as the crisis ebbs, her need for you decreases.

This is never to be a co-dependent relationship, but she can't walk all over you and do whatever she pleases. Require mutual respect—you extend respect to her but she must also reciprocate. Sharing your life with others is a gift to be treasured. However, do not expect her to hang on your every word.

People walk into your life with baggage. Some not only carry their own but they've been handed suitcases from others as well. Damaged and disheartened, they cling to a wisp of faith but the lies from their past haunt them. Developing a mentor relationship with them is delicate business.

They want what you have to offer but unpacking those bags can become too painful. So they stay stuck, or worse, they leave. They are captured by their choices. They are heavily weighted down with all they carry. Their hands are so full, they cannot hold onto God's promises.

This is happened to me a few times. What do you do when your love and commitment is not enough? I know, it's so hard. But you have to let them go and give them over to God.

When You Don't Know What To Do

James 1:5 teaches to pray for wisdom. As a mentor, you should be consistently and even constantly praying for wisdom. Your words and, even more so, your actions hold weight in the eyes of the young people in your life. You cannot manipulate or guilt them to stay in a relationship with you. Especially when you see them heading for failure. If they make a poor choice, you can voice your opinion but be careful: perhaps only do this once and only if it is asked for. Sometimes, you have to let them fail. Failure is a powerful teacher.

Wow, that is so hard. It's so hard to watch them go down, when you could see it coming a mile away but they wouldn't listen. I know. But sometimes that's the only way they can learn. I don't suppose you ever had any of those moments when you were younger, did you?

Notice in Philippians, Paul reminds us to work out our own salvation: "Dear friends, you always followed my instructions when I was with you. And now that I am away, it is even more important. Work hard to show the results of your salvation, obeying God with deep reverence and fear" (Philippians 2:12 NLT). It takes hard work. There are no simple solutions. We each need to invest time and effort to move forward.

Paul encourages the Christians in Philippi to continue to develop their relationship with God (Philippians 2:12). He couldn't tell them how to live every moment of every day. They had to do it on their own. Treat your young friends in the same way. I know, that is fine and easy when it's working and glorifying God...but sometimes missteps have to happen. In turn, they will understand the real grace Jesus has imparted to them. Sometimes you have to let them fall. If they allow, help wipe off the dirt and bandage their cuts and bruises. Learning the hard way imparts lessons they don't forget.

Wouldn't it be nice if mentoring was like coaching someone through a maze? Standing above, you can see all the obstacles in the runner's way. You could yell out, "no, turn left. Yes! Go straight there!" Would that be great? At the end, with your help, your mentee successfully made it through. But, did they learn anything? Could they repeat the exact same path without your help? Would they understand the grave consequences of making a wrong turn? Probably not. This is a silly example, but an apt metaphor—you must let them work through issues on their own terms. They need to recognize they have a voice and Jesus hears them. They need to understand it is the Lord they need to find dependence on—not you.

Power Tools

> Prayer is the most powerful tool a mentor possesses.

One young friend broke off meeting with me soon after she became engaged. Deep in her spirit she feared I didn't approve of this young man. The truth was I didn't. I felt she was entering marriage for the wrong reasons. I never had the opportunity to share that opinion with her, though I fear my words would not have made a difference anyway. She was determined to follow through with her own desires. I did however, pray. I prayed for God's truth, I prayed for her eyes to be opened to the reality of her situation. Amazingly, they were and she broke off the engagement. I certainly was not the only one praying for her, but I know the prayers made a difference, even though I didn't get to speak with her.

Prayer is the most powerful tool a mentor possesses. Prayer works when words fail. You don't always get the outcome you are seeking. Prayer surrenders the situation to God. It gets you out of the way and allows Him to work.

Second, you have the power of encouragement. Cheer them on when they make good choices. Acknowledge their perseverance, especially when they want to give up. Let them know you will be there, no matter what their actions. You are on their side even when you don't like what they are doing. You will love them no matter who they are or what they do, because Jesus does.

Third, you can let them go in love. Forcing a friendship or mentorship will only lead to feeling trapped for both you and her. False expectations arise, and your mentee can fall into playing a role instead of being themselves. They lose their authenticity, which leads to bitterness. They begin to hate the community of people that require them to fit into a specific mold. Instead of bringing freedom it loads on more baggage.

By letting go, you give permission to make mistakes. This isn't enabling them to sin, but giving freedom to find grace. This freedom allows them to turn to Jesus and ask Him what He wants them to do. It forces them to take responsibility for their own life. It may be the single most important step they take. It can be a huge step of faith or the biggest mistake of their lives. Either way, you have to let them take it. It's actually an act of love on your part.

I would rather my young friend take ownership of their life—you're teaching her how to be an adult. Mistakes will happen, and when they do, adults say "I'm doing this and the results are my responsibility." Even if the act is childish and wrong, taking responsibility for it is a step in the right direction.

The Pain of the Wayward

You can see her defining moment. She has come to a fork in the road; one way is clearly out of God's will and it is the one she chooses. You saw it coming a mile away. She knows it wrong but the temptation was too great. She lets you go with her for a while but your presence whispers the truth. She leaves you behind, assuring you she is fine. You must let the prodigal go.

> He loves them more—more than we can imagine.

You are not God. I know you know that, but sometimes you feel you must do something. It is out of your control. I know, I don't like that either. So what do you do? Practice what you preach, and turn to Jesus. Look to Him and trust Him. Pray for your young friend that Jesus uses the experience to build her and your faith and trust in Him. Remember, she is His creation; yes, you love her, but He loves her more. Stop for a moment and really let that sink in. He loves them more—more than we can imagine.

Luke 15:11-32 tells us the story of the lost son. You love and wait, and pray for new relationships to come into their life to bring them back to Jesus. Your friendship with them is not as important as their relationship with Jesus. ALWAYS remember this: Jesus is standing and watching the road waiting for His young one to return.

Perhaps this isn't happening with your mentee, but with a wayward son or daughter. Their choices have brought anguish and though it is out of your control, you want to do something to bring them back. Your frustration makes you say something stupid and the rift between you grows larger and larger until there seems to be no way back. But Jesus knows your child. He sees it all and still loves both of you. He never gives up, He never stops waiting at the end the road watching for the lost one. He loves your son or daughter more than you do. I know it's hard to fathom because a mother's love is so huge. But He does. Trust Him and pray.

Prayer is the powerful tool God has given us to fight evil and draw your loved one back home.

Lord I lift the sorrowing mom reading this right now to you. As she reads this page, help her find peace, perseverance, and patience. Bring her young one home. In Jesus' Name, amen. For Everything A Season

There is another kind of letting go—when the need for mentoring diminishes. The relationship continues but the mentoring ebbs. That's okay, and sometimes even a great thing! We remember Ecclesiastes 3:5-6—

"A time to scatter stones and a time to gather stones.

A time to embrace and a time to turn away.

A time to search and a time to quit searching.

A time to keep and a time to throw away."

There is a time for everything. I live in Michigan, and I love that we have four distinct seasons. Fall, winter, spring, and summer each have their own beauty. (It would be nice if someone reminded me of that come February, though.) They say if you don't like the weather here, wait five minutes and it will change.

Ministry feels that way sometimes. Any interaction with people has one ironic constant—that of change.

Starting relationships and letting go has a constant flow of change—but one that is necessary if the church is to continue in the next generation. This includes knowing when you are to step aside for others to shine. Change. It is not an age thing; it is all about passion and God's timing. God will energize you into your senior years, if he called you there. He calls every one to ministry, but when it is time for someone new your energy will recede.

No matter where you are in your service, look for your replacement. I led the Women's Ministry at my church for a number of years. The last eighteen months brought more fatigue than passion. I knew it was time to change, so I began training the next leader. I knew it was time to hand it completely to her when I found myself responding to new ideas in this manner.

"That is not how we do things." Or "We've tried that, it didn't work." I saw the confusion and disappointment on others' faces when I said such things. I realized this was not Kingdom building—this is being stuck. It was time for new blood to run through that ministry. As I've stepped back I have not stepped out. Sarah, the new leader, and I still meet on a regular basis. Now I'm the encourager. It is a delight to see her shine in this new position. Her ideas have reinvigorated a ministry that had plateaued. I wasn't doing a bad job, it just needed new life. New life I couldn't give it. Change I couldn't facilitate.

As a mentor, you must be aware of circumstances in young friend's life, and when it is time to make a change. There is a time to step back and let them go. Even in our families—none of us want our children to live with us forever. We want them to move out and into their own life. It's not always easy, but it is important they live individual lives. You will find this to be true for your protégé as well. It doesn't mean you aren't friends anymore. It just means your relationship will change. Recognize the time and let go—it is a healthy and a happy parting of ways.

Dear Lord, I pray for wisdom for each of us to understand our role in another's life. Give us knowledge that will guide us through this process. Give us courage to know when to let go. We trust you with these relationships and ask that they are centered on You. In Jesus Name, AMEN.

Questions:

1. What are some ways you can test to see if you have found the right person to mentor?

2. Read Philippians 2:12. How does this help you deal other's poor choices?

3. Why is prayer so important in these relationships?

4. Why is it important to know everything has a season?

Chapter Eleven: Spiritual Motherhood

When first married, I wanted a big family—a house full of kids! Adoption seemed like a real possibility. Then after our three kids came, we had a miscarriage and I was tired. It seemed that a family of five is all I could handle. Dreams of adoption vaporized in the crazy days of raising young children. Yet, I always knew there was more to our family than the five of us.

Truth be told, my image was idealistic. I didn't understand the stress of another human's 24/7 dependence. I have dealt with a lot of poop, pee, and puke in the last 22 years. (More so in the beginning, in case you are concerned.) Of course, I also didn't understand the joy of giggles and snuggles either. As I look back now, I see we were caught up in our own little family. Now as we approach the empty nest, I'm glad we chose it this way.

It wasn't until I started writing today, that I realized God answered my wish for a big family through spiritual parenting. It was a seed the Lord planted a long time ago but I didn't understand exactly how it would grow. The young women in my life are dear to me—they're like my own children. They are an important part of my life. Like my own kids, their love is a joy.

Spiritual Kids

These relationships develop slowly. They need to be nourished and developed. Not all people in your life will become family. As a mentor, be open to the idea that they might bust open your heart and even house. "Enlarge your house; build an addition. Spread out your home, and spare no expense! For you will soon be bursting at the seams. Your descendants will occupy other nations and resettle the ruined cities" (Isaiah 54:2-3 NLT).

Your descendants aren't just your biological children. Spiritual children can also be part of our homes. Are you prepared to accept new "daughters" into your life?

Whether or not you have biological kids, when you mentor, you have spiritual kids. You don't even have to be married! The relationship with your younger friend becomes much like mothering—your nurturing instincts kick in and she becomes your spiritual child.

This is exactly how Paul describes his relationship with Timothy—"my true child in the faith," he writes (I Timothy 1:2 NLT). This is a unique situation, because from what we know of Timothy, his father did not share the same faith. Paul wasn't a replacement, but an enrichment.

More than likely, your young friend will already have her own mother, and you will not be a replacement—nor should you be. But your spiritual motherhood is an enrichment in her life, and in yours as well.

I wanted to call this chapter Spirit Momma. But that sounds too

much like something out of a Disney movie. Then I thought, Spiritual Parenting—but that sounds so formal. In reality, this relationship somewhere in between both. It's not ideal, it's not conventional. But it certainly is impactful.

Be careful here, though, to not overwhelm yourself or put your biological family in danger of sacrifice. Mentoring is never about numbers; quantity is never the goal. Invite in only the number of young women you personally can handle. Prayerfully ask God how big to make your "tent." Start with one adopted daughter at a time. As you settle into that relationship pursue the next. Or you may never add another young person to your life. Never sacrifice your family for mentoring. And keep in mind some people need more time and attention than others.

Spiritual parenting is not literally raising a child. However, it reflects important aspects of it, particularly when it comes to love. Love your spiritual children unconditionally. While you may choose to dislike some of their behaviors, never reject the individual. Paul set this example for us in his letter to the Thessalonians. Examine the familial language Paul uses; "For you know that we dealt with each of you as a father deals with his own children, encouraging, comforting and urging you to live lives worthy of God, who calls you into his kingdom and glory" (I Thessalonians 2:11-12 NIV).

"As a father deals with his own children." The apostle Paul made it clear these relationships are strong and long-lasting, much like a parent's relationship should be. Work to form a bond that lasts. This is not a short-term commitment. Put simply, it means you will be there for them. Demonstrate to them that they matter. They matter to you like your biological kids matter to you.

What does it mean to encourage, comfort, and urge? To encourage someone it means to give them courage to take the next step. When they falter, motivate them to move forward.

For example, one of my young friends was thrown into a leadership position while on a mission trip. She was given no warning and was only a little older than the team she was leading. She did have experience, and she is a trained leader in our church. When she called in a panic, her initial response was to give up and come home. So I asked her questions:

"Did God call you on this trip?"

"I think so?"

"Do you have experience and training you can share?"

"I guess, but I'm scared."

"That's good. It will keep you dependent on God. You can do this."

"Thanks. Pray for me."

I did not give her much advice. I simply asked those questions and told her I believed in her. I assured her I would pray and I did. In fact the intercession that week was heavy and constant. I did not know what was ahead of her, and neither did she! Once she was overseas, I could not communicate with her, so I too, had to trust Jesus to walk her through this adventure. It turned out to be a challenging trip. But God showed up and God led her. She was strengthened by the experience and now has greater courage!

Encourage but also comfort. Although this generation is more globally aware, they are still somewhat naïve. They can be blindsided by life when it doesn't go as they plan or expect. Transitioning into adulthood has not gotten easier since I did it (however many years ago that was!). Understanding relationships, making decisions on careers, and establishing independence can be overwhelming. Disappointments occur and your young friends need comfort. They need a safe place to share their fears. Affirm their feelings and point them toward the truth of their situation. This is not a time for advice—it's a time to reassure them God has a plan. It is a time to demonstrate faithfulness. They can walk away from you but you will not abandon them. And neither will God.

Sometimes it is through their discomfort you can urge them to make the right choices. Lead by example, just as Jesus did (see John 13:15). When your young friends get caught up in a tough circumstance, remind them of the big picture. We all live for God's Kingdom and His glory. Remind them you too, are imperfect—honesty about your flaws demonstrates your authenticity—but you're determined to seek after God's own heart as best you can. They are to do the same.

When life is hard, console and comfort them. Bad things happen to all of us: death, illness, and accidents steal from us. They absorb joy and drive us to despair. Comfort is imperative. Your quiet presence can make the difference in ways you may not understand. Be there for your friend when they experience loss. This gentle act of kindness touches the soul.

As a spiritual mom, urge your children to live a life reflective of Jesus. Urge is a strong word. The Greek word used in I Thessalonians 2:12 is, martureo,[1] literally meaning to live as witnesses. Aspire to live as a

> You can do this because He is in you; Jesus is all you need.

witness, as well as inspire a life that daily gives testimony to the Holy Spirit in you. This is a tall order and cannot be done without His empowerment. Don't let this scare you into disqualifying yourself. No—let it inspire you to take the next step of faith. You can do this because IIc is in you; Jesus is all you need. Let His perfect love drive out the fear that wants to creep in (see I John 4:18).

Scripture teaches you are part of God's family and to help one another. Just like you are present for your biological family, be present for your spiritual family. "Therefore, whenever we have the opportunity, we should do good to everyone—especially to those in the family of faith" (Galatians 6:10 NLT). You have an inheritance given to you by God. His Spirit empowers you to reach out and welcome them into your "tent." Paul expounds on this in Colossians: "We also pray that you will be strengthened with all his glorious power so you will have all the endurance and patience you need. May you be filled with joy, always thanking the Father. He has enabled you to share in the inheritance that belongs to his people, who live in the light" (Colossians 1:11-12 NLT). What a delight to share this inheritance with others—learn to build them up to strengthen your community. It's exciting to be part of such growth.

There is no set time or program for mentoring or spiritual parenting. Meet as long as it benefits your young friend; remember—this relationship is not about you. Your goal is to become their spiritual parent. Would you ask your children how long they would like you to be their mother? I know the lack of structure can be frustrating at times, and you may wonder what you're getting into. But you may need a paradigm shift—mentoring is sometimes more than just ministry or an act of service. You may be in it for the long haul (see I John 3:16).

> When it gets difficult, remind yourself that unconditional love comes through us from Jesus.

I see these individuals as lifelong friends. Their need for me will diminish over time but my love for them is there for good. I want to nurture a relationship that will last a lifetime. When it gets difficult, remind yourself that unconditional love comes through us from Jesus. He is the unquenchable source of your love for others, and as such, there is never a lack of supply. Jesus' love is what empowers you to give up your lives for others.

Having said that, I'm sure you already know that all of life is a balancing act. You have other responsibilities that need your attention. Building a mentoring relationship does not mean you are to be available 24-7, and it's important that you determine your boundaries and stick to them.

In times of crisis, however, you do need to make yourself available. Spontaneous calls, texts, or requests for meetings can happen. Talk with them and determine the seriousness of their situation. It may only take a short phone call. They may only need to be heard. Or maybe you need to meet and hash some things out. Either way, be a sounding board and let them verbally vomit. Then, after listening (and only after listening), ask them how you can help them. Do they want your advice? Most of the time, I've found, advice is not what they are looking for. They need someone safe to vent their frustrations. You are there to support them. Get to know the personality of your mentee. Do they have a tendency for drama? Are they understated? Understanding them as individuals will give you a measuring stick for your response.

Develop a relationship that feels like family. This can be tricky because none of us truly know what a perfectly healthy family looks like. Remember, this is a family that reflects the love of Jesus. Perfection is not the goal, but love is our measuring tool. We follow Paul's advice to Timothy: "Treat older women as you would your mother, and treat younger women with all purity as you would your own sisters" (I Timothy 5:2, NLT). Behave in a way that is respectful and treat them in a respectful manner.

That Time Elijah Got A Son

Elijah did many great things a prophet of God. But in I Kings 19 we see that he is worn out and fed up with serving Israel. God responds to Elijah's despondence by sending him to Elisha. Elisha was to be Elijah's replacement, and an interesting relationship grew. Elijah was abrupt with Elisha. Elijah was getting old and tired. But

Elisha hung on because he knew the gift he was gaining by spending time with the prophet.

As Elijah prepared to leave, Elisha asked for a "double portion of his spirit" (see II Kings 2:9). Elisha was specifically requesting to be Elijah's replacement. The double portion inheritance always went to the eldest son in accordance with Mosaic Law. This son was then expected to carry on his father's business and maintain his properties. But get this—Elisha's request wasn't just asking for a double of Elijah's gift, or a cut of the will. He was requesting to be regarded as Elijah's son. And not just any son, but the firstborn son. It was a huge request, steeped in Hebrew tradition, but reflective of the importance of their relationship. With this title would come not only the responsibility of the prophet but also the respect of the prophet.

Actually, this was not Elijah's choice. Only God could ordain his successor: "'You have asked a difficult thing,' Elijah replied. 'If you see me when I am taken from you, then you will get your request. But if not, then you won't'" (II Kings 2:10 NLT).

Three times Elijah tried to send Elisha away, but Elisha refused to leave. Elisha knew this was Elijah's last day on earth. Such loyalty does not happen by chance; It is evident in true and dependable relationships. This was a reliable mentorship. Elisha was determined to stay with Elijah to the end.

Spoiler alert: Elisha saw him, he received his spirit and he continued Elijah's work.

Learn three important Biblical principles here: one, your successors are to be like sons and daughters to you; two, God chooses your successors; and three, loyalty develops a true friendship.

We don't see much of the relationship of Elijah and Elisha, only the results. However, we can imagine what it looked like based on

Hebrew traditions in Scripture. Parents were encouraged to teach God's ways to their children throughout their day. This was done through discussion as well as example.

Deuteronomy 11:19 (NLT) says "Teach them to your children. Talk about them when you are at home and when you are on the road, when you are going to bed and when you are getting up." This is really how others learn from you. It's not sitting in a lecture hall listening to profound wisdom, but living life together. You teach as you influence others by your life. So let them see how you live; welcome your young friends into your home, invite them to serve with you in ministry, attend events they are passionate about, and share meals.

You might even teach them a skill you enjoy (Titus 2). I have often taught young women to cook. We find a day that works and they hang with me while I make a meal. They help prep, cook, and then eat it. Another skill I love is reading, and with some we discuss the latest book I've read.

Mentoring is more than sharing Scriptural tenants. It is laughing, crying, and loving.

> Mentoring is more than sharing Scriptural tenants. It is laughing, crying, and loving.

It's God's job to determine what your friend will get out of your relationship, and we have to trust God with it. You don't have to guess how to best train them; God will give you insight as you ask for it (you are asking for it, right?) "For the Lord grants wisdom! From his mouth come knowledge and understanding" (Proverbs 2:6 NLT). God will direct your path. It may not be as dramatic as Elisha's assurance from Elijah but it will come. Trust God with it. He will show you! And remember—it's His choice.

Be a true and trustworthy friend. "There are "friends" who destroy each other, but a real friend sticks closer than a brother" (Proverbs 18:24 NLT). Your mentoring relationship has a goal, and that goal is to develop a stable, reliable relationship. Your mentee becomes like a daughter.

Loyalty and Confidence

I have heard things like...

"You are the only one I've told."

"I needed someone I could call that wouldn't freak out"

"I need you to give your honest opinion about this."

I am always stunned when one of my young friends confides in me this way. It is an honor.

Of course, they didn't say those things the first time we met. I had to prove myself before they were at a point they could tell me things that would be preceded by those phrases! We have to show ourselves to be loyal and people of integrity. You can do this! Yes, it is a tall order but you have the Holy Spirit residing in you. He has empowered you to do His will.

You must always keep their confidence. They need to know that when you hear something from them. It goes nowhere else. PERIOD. Your job is to guard their heart. Trusted information is just that—trusted to you to keep it safe. It is not a source of gossip or prayer requests to share with others. Exceptions occur only in life-threatening situations—when you see immediate danger to them or to those around them.

Once, I blurted out one of these facts shared with me in confidence. To my credit, I did not know I was the only one she had shared her celebratory news. She had gotten into the college of her choice and I assumed it was general knowledge. In a group of people, I made a comment about her achievement. She quickly pulled me aside and informed me that no one else knew. OOPS! It had the potential to ruin all we had built together. Thankfully, no harm was done, and I profusely apologized. She was not upset, but it was a lesson learned on my part. Never reveal information shared with you unless you know it is okay with the other person. Even good news. It is theirs to discuss and yours to support.

"A friend is always loyal, and a brother is born to help in time of need" (Proverbs 17:17 NLT).

The Hebrew word used for loyal here is ahab. It means to have human love for another or friendship. A friend loves at all times, therefore they are loyal. When life gets difficult, this friend does not abandon. They stay. This kind of friendship is steadfast, with firm and constant support.

So the next question is, can you be an unwavering friend? Keep in mind you can disagree with an action without leaving the friendship. It's easy to be quick to judge and to shame, but you cannot do that in mentoring relationships. Given the opportunity, express your opinion about an action but do not condemn them. Your opinion is important to them. "The heartfelt counsel of a friend is as sweet as perfume and incense" (Proverbs 27:9 NLT). That's how I want my young friends to view me. My counsel, not my judgment, is in their best interest. It refreshes them, even in correction.

Working with millennials can feel like your loyalty is one-sided. It is difficult to stay devoted to them when their devotion seems to wane. For this generation, trust is difficult. Their lack of trust undermines their unstable loyalty. I can't blame them we have brought them up in an unstable world. But what you may not realize is they still respect you. They may have wandered away, broken appointments, and not returned your calls, but that does not mean they don't want you in their life. Correct this behavior, teach them the proper responses.

Remind yourself to model the correct behavior; be fiercely loyal, and remember it's not about you. You are a stable influence, not a wounded friend. Be flexible, but not a doormat; give them a time frame to meet or talk. Set boundaries, but not too many. You're developing a friendship, not a military unit. Communicate you are available. Invite

> Point them to Jesus through your loyalty.

them into your life but willingly accept no. Answer their texts and take their calls. Of course there are times you can't talk, but let them know when you are available and that you want to hear them.

Caring for the next generation takes understanding. It's hard for them to know where they can find stable ground. Point them to Jesus through your loyalty.

As with any relationship, one or the other will do things that may hurt or disappoint. This is why Jesus must be in the center. "Make allowance for each other's faults, and forgive anyone who offends you. Remember, the Lord forgave you, so you must forgive others" (Colossians 3:13 NLT). That pretty much sums it up. The Lord forgave you, you should forgive others—enough said.

Newsflash: You're not perfect. You won't be, and they won't be, either. If you are at fault, be quick to ask for forgiveness. Use the words, "will you forgive me for…" to be clear you are humbly asking for forgiveness. In turn, live in a state of forgiveness toward your friend. Don't wait for them to ask for it, just give it. Live a life of grace—it is contagious.

Like Family

I have one young friend who occasionally stays with us. It is not because she doesn't have a home, but because we are closer to her college campus than her family. When she is here, she is one of ours. She shares our meal time, relaxes with the family and has free use of the laundry room

> Live a life of grace—it is contagious.

and kitchen. She is respectful of our home and doesn't take advantage of us. There are missteps on both our parts at times but most of all there is love—and grace.

At times these relationships are inconvenient, but they are never a burden. My to-do list has to be set aside so I can give one of my young friends my complete attention. You might have to do the same. They need you when they are sick. They need you when they've had a relationship crisis, and they need you when they don't have a relationship. They need you when they have a financial issues, when they lose their jobs, change majors, or feel like quitting school. They don't need you to fix their problems, but so they know they are not alone. It sounds like a huge commitment, and in some ways, it is. But it's really no different than any other friendship. Simply put, just be there for them.

They also need you in quiet times. If you haven't heard from them, it is time to reach out. A quick text of "How are you?" or "How can I pray for you?" is all you need to do. Their life can get hectic. This outreach reminds them they are important to you, you haven't forgotten about them, and they are not alone. Even when life is great for them, it's a wonderful reminder you are there for them. Don't take it personally if they don't respond, and don't give up. Try again at another time.

This world is lonely, amplified by divorce and dysfunction. Many of our young friends are broken and they don't even know why. Often it has nothing to do with their own choices but choices by others around them. But Jesus loves to take our brokenness, mend us, make

> But Jesus loves to take our brokenness, mend us, make us new, and use us to build others up through Him. We must continually point to Jesus.

us new, and use us to build others up through Him. We must continually point to Jesus.

Most of the energy for mentoring is not directed at their problems but at accepting them for who they are now. I spend time praying for them. Lifting up specific requests and praying for their relationship with God. I treat them like I would want others to treat my children. My kids have had powerful mentors—people who loved them unconditionally, whose insight was a little different than mine. Their faith has developed and grown because of it. We need each other, and I am so thankful for the positive input these people have had in my kids' lives.

You do have to be sensitive to them and the other relationships in their life. Not all are healthy, and you can't assume everyone will respond to them as you do or respond well to your relationship with them. You are not superior to others; fight the urge to judge those who make your young friends' lives difficult. It's easy to take on an offense for them, but you can't—it's not your role. It's tempting to fight their injustices, but you are not their savior. You may need to re-read that last sentence. Here it is again: You are not their savior.

Sometimes, they will look at you as if you are infallible. "What do you think God is telling me?" The look on their face is comical when I say I don't know. "But you are so wise!" they say in bewilderment. "Thank you," I reply. "But I don't have a secret access to God's throne room. We all enter the same way—Jesus." It's better to teach them to hear for themselves than to listen for them. So I usually answer their question with a question "What do you think?"

Jesus taught this way, by asking good questions. Keep challenging your young friend to think and search and yearn for the voice of God. Never are you to replace God's voice with your own. Remind them that they, too can go boldly into the throne room of God through Jesus.

I know that you know you are not God and would never want to put yourself in that position. That's just common sense. But. Women of a certain age (ugh, my age!) want to feel needed. It builds our ego to be admired, doesn't it? But be careful not to think too highly of yourself. It will trip you up. (See Proverbs 16:18.) Pride will creep in. Be on guard. If your friend puts you on a pedestal, be aware enough to climb back down before you fall off. (Because you will fall off.)

> God is the source for all you need to move forward in this position.

God is the source for all you need to move forward in this position. I love that! As you meet with Him, He fills you with all you need. Well, let's be honest—all you need is Him. The thought will (or probably already has) cross your mind, "but I need more wisdom, I need more time, I need more love." My friend, God is the source of all of that. Trust Him to lead you through this and provide all you need. Too prideful? He will provide humility. Too doubtful? He will provide faith. Too self-centered? He will provide altruism. He is the source of all things good and you have free access to all He has to offer.

We will make mistakes. And in fact, a mistake is an improvement over not acting at all! Present it back to God with a humble heart and He will work it out for His good. (Romans 8:28). In your imperfection, He moves through you and builds others up. You may wibble-wobble through life but He makes your path straight. He who is in you is greater! Remember, memorize, and whisper this simple prayer: "I trust you, Jesus, to take me through."

I am so thankful for His daily direction!

Step out in faith, find your spiritual daughter. Together you will learn God's plan for your relationship.

> Live life together.
> Grow your family.
> Leave a legacy.

Oh, and one more thing—don't forget to laugh. See the humor in life. Life is more than struggles and stresses. Take time to have fun, and don't be afraid to be silly. Sometimes we need to lighten up and enjoy ourselves. Live life together. Grow your family. Leave a legacy.

Lord: I lift up my friend reading these pages today. May you bring life to your direction in her heart. May she see the importance of becoming a spiritual parent. Oh Lord, give each of us eyes to see Your Kingdom. Help us to know who to connect with and then what to do once we are connected. Teach us to be friends that are trustworthy and true. Give us opportunity to live life as an example that invites others to join in and be a part of it. Give us YOUR wisdom each day so we will know how to influence others in your purpose. We come against fear, in Jesus name, and pray for courage to take on this role. We pray for your Holy Spirit empowerment to take us to the depth of relationships that you want us to pursue. In Jesus Name, AMEN

Questions:

1. What does it mean to enlarge your "tent"?

2. What does matureo mean? How does this apply to mentoring?

3. What is it important to live a life of grace in spiritual parenting?

Chapter Twelve—Christ, Coffee, and Caring

It all started with a simple instruction. If they call and ask you to talk, say yes. Keep your calendar open. You are to make time for this. Make yourself available. Never did I dream that when I said yes to this instruction, I would open a new ministry.

One afternoon, my phone rattled with a text message. I was in the middle of painting my front entryway. It was still summer, but my fall semester was starting soon and lessons needed to be planned. I was finishing summer projects and preparing for the school year.

Ugh I have so much to do – should I even look? I thought.

"Can we meet for coffee this week?" She wrote.

Deadlines were approaching and her text panicked me a bit.

"Lord, yes, we are called to teach the younger generation does it have to be this week?" I prayed. "Okay, okay, I'll say yes."

Later that week we sat across from each other. As she sipped coffee, she leaned in toward me, and I knew today had nothing to do with coffee. This dear young woman simply needed to share her heart. Big decisions loomed in her life; barely 23, she had choices to make. She passionately poured out all the thoughts swirling around in her head. It seemed to lay on the table between us in a tangled mess. She talked, I simply had to listen. By the end of our coffee cups she had determined her next step. Although she still had concerns, she was convinced of her path. It wasn't on my original agenda for the week, but it was time well spent.

Time Well Spent

Titus 2 clearly instructs older women to teach younger women, and older men to teach younger men (it's not just a woman thing). The scriptural directive still holds true although the methods have changed. You have an opportunity to influence the coming generation. Make yourself available, approachable, and adaptable, and listen to the hearts of these young women. Believe it or not, they desperately want to talk to you! There is a hunger for the younger generation to connect with the older generation. They want to be heard.

They want to be reassured and valued. They want your friendship. Yes, this involves a cost. It involves your time. But isn't it worth it? The next generation needs to stand on your shoulders to better see where they need to go.

I don't meet with them often. No more than once a month. I see them at church or even run into them in public. Yes, there are phone calls and texts. There are occasional Facebook posts and messages, but all of it is worth it. When I first started mentoring, my coffee meetings lasted about an hour. Now they can go for three...because I enjoy them!

It's Not About The Coffee

I love coffee. There, I said it. It is my favorite hello first thing in the morning. Give me a cup of coffee and I am your friend. I enjoy the taste and the caffeine doesn't hurt either. It is a comfort, a familiar friend. Which is why I often meet friends at coffeehouses. However, when it comes to mentoring, the coffee doesn't really matter. I know, I can't believe I wrote that either.

We have met in my home and their home, at church, in parks, and we've gone for walks. The location doesn't matter. It's nice to have something to do; coffee is a social nicety, coffee shops are cute, and as it has been established—I like coffee. So it works.

I usually let them choose the meeting place; I want them to be comfortable. If they are uncertain, I will make some suggestions, initially a public place, and usually a coffeehouse. The millennials love coffee! But it's okay if you don't. Beverages are the tool, not the point.

These coffee meetings take on the personality of my mentee with a little dash of me. I let them direct the content of our conversation but I help the conversation with open ended questions like "What did you want to talk about today?" and "Why do you think or feel that?" or "How can I help you?" Some will come with a paper with points listed to make sure they cover everything while others meander through the conversation with ease. Our conversations vary from light to serious. We share laughter and, at times, tears. Even on my most difficult days, the appointments delight me.

Now it is your turn. It doesn't have to be coffee for you—it could be anything, like running, or biking, or baking, or whatever it is you might like to do with your mentee. But here's the thing—you have to do it.

Set a time to meet. You haven't spent one-on-one time with this person before…what goes through your mind? Yes, I know, what to wear? I know this because I face the dilemma that frustrates women across America daily. It is the age old struggle of womanhood. What to wear? As much as we hate to admit it, it plays a role in our life every morning. The clothes we put on reflect a bit of our personality.

Don't laugh, but one time before I met with a new friend one time I peered into my closet with this age-old struggle of womanhood. (I'm fairly certain even Eve had a hard time deciding on which fig leaves to wear back in the day.) So always looking to impress, I donned a red V-neck T-shirt and jeans, finishing the whole outfit with my snazzy sneakers. The image wasn't exactly impressive.

But here's the deal—your clothes don't matter. Don't get caught up in the external—either for you or her.

Don't be put off by what they look like. The tattoos, the piercings, the beards, the clothes, they are all decorations. Have you seen gauges? They kind of freak me out. Tongue piercings? Yuck! But remember, none of these are reflective of their heart. These adornments don't mean the same thing as they did when we were young. For most of them it is self-expression and fashion. They are making a statement: "I am an individual, and I'm not like you. Take time to hear me."

> Your relationship with Christ determines your identity and your confidence.

And yes, mentoring a millennial can be intimidating, but the best way to make a good first impression is to be yourself! Seriously—that is all you have to do. If you are comfortable in your own skin, the clothes don't matter. It is better to remember to come dressed with these attributes:

confidence (Jeremiah 17:7)—Your relationship with Christ determines your identity and your confidence. If you are not there yet, pursue Jesus. He will meet you. Your confidence ebbs and flows but He is steadfast. He WILL pick you up when you fall.

humility (Ephesians 4:2)—You don't have all the answers. Recognize your own inadequacy but give what you have. "Always be humble and gentle. Be patient with each other, making allowance for each others' faults because of your love" (Ephesians 4:2 NLT). And, don't forget—I Peter 5:5 says that God gives grace to the humble!

authenticity (2 Timothy 2:2)—Be yourself. Recognize you are characterized by what you do, not by how you appear. Be authentic; don't try to put up a front or a false identity.

Just Listen

The younger generation needs you to listen now. Here are what a few of these young women said about our meetings.

"[I appreciate] being able to talk about anything and everything that is happening in my life. Whether it's good or bad, I know that I can confide in her and that she will offer me Biblical advice and her unconditional love and support." – Caitlin, 24

"[I appreciate] being listened to without being judged. Having someone who knows me and knows my life situations but still has an objective opinion. I also value the consistency, I can literally call freaking out and I don't have to over explain the whole situation because my mentor already knows it from being in contact on a regular basis." – Annie, 25

Listen first, and pray. You can comment, but that is not as important as your presence. Invest your time. Your words can fertilize their journey but they are not the source of their sustenance. Too often, it's easy to be ready with advice, thinking experience trumps their youthful enthusiasm. However, many of these young people are in tune with the Holy Spirit, but they need a sounding board they can trust to unravel what can appear to be mysterious. Not until they ask for your advice should you give it. Delivered too soon, the advice will go unheard.

You also don't want to send them in the wrong direction with a quick expression of your opinion. You may not realize it but when you speak they hang on your words. If you're not sure what is the best answer, it's much better to say, "I don't know" or "I'm not sure" than to blurt out the first thing that comes to mind.

My natural tendency is to speak first, and I have to guard against this. That is why I love the book of James, especially James 1:19 (NLT): "Understand this, my dear brothers and sisters: You must all be quick to listen, slow to speak, and slow to get angry." As a mentor your words hold weight. You developed and nurtured a trust relationship with your young friends. A thoughtless objection could erode that trust.

If she asks for your advice, she wants your opinion. This opinion needs to be expressed out of humility and wisdom not a quick, proud response. Many times they already know what God is telling them, and they just need affirmation or helping thinking it through. Ask them to express what God has already communicated to them. Through a series of questions, they find the answer. This is delicate ground, especially if they don't like what they have heard from you— or what you have affirmed.

Words of Wisdom

James also reminds us to ask for wisdom (James 1:5). If we ask, God will give it to us. The millennial generation speaks with bravado. Brazen comments can appear disrespectful when the source is passion. Gentle rebukes are received only once the trust is established.

This takes time. Be patient—let the fruits of the Spirit grow and emit from you. Nurture those and you will nurture others.

As you grow to know one another you may recognize a need for correction. Listen with intention to understand. Is there an underlying concern that needs to be unearthed? Do you notice red flags? Instead of an interjection of correction, I make a mental note to pray over that area. Many times, I ask the Holy Spirit for His opinion. If correction is needed, I ask Him to lead the way as to when to speak and when to pray.

Before you address it with your friend, first look at yourself. This isn't easy or comfortable, but it is necessary, as Luke 6 instructs: "How can you think of saying, 'Friend, let me help you get rid of that speck in your eye,' when you can't see past the log in your own eye? Hypocrite! First get rid of the log in your own eye; then you will see well enough to deal with the speck in your friend's eye" (Luke 6:42 NLT).

Ask yourself:

> Wait on the Lord to see if there is something from your past He is working on through this relationship.

Have I contributed to their lack of fruit?

Am I communicating clearly?

Am I flexible?

Am I authentic?

Am I too pushy or to lax?

Prayerfully respond to each of these questions. Wait on the Lord to see if there is something from your past He is working on through this relationship. Journal your thoughts or write down your answers.

Take responsibility for any of your contribution and begin the process to correct them. You may even consider sharing this with someone to keep you accountable in your efforts.

Take a look at your personalities, and note any personality difference. Make sure the issue you're seeing red flags about isn't your personal preference in growth in the Lord. Perhaps you're just seeing a generation gap. How much of it is a really fruitlessness and how much is missteps due to lack of understanding? Lay down your expectations and honestly look at the relationship.

It could be a maturity issue. Your young friend (emphasis on the young) may not have experienced an accountable relationship before. It may take new boundaries to be put in place. Rarely do I ask for specific goals from my mentee, but if you see a repeating pattern of immaturity, this could be helpful. But make sure these "mentoring rules" are always heavily weighted with grace.

If you determine a change needs to occur and you should say something, this must be done in person. Set a meeting time. If she's evasive, explain to her you have some concerns that need to be addressed and it needs to be done in person. Do not address these by email or text—it just gets confusing and it's so hard to communicate your heart with just words on a screen. If she refuses to set a time, tell her it is time to sever the mentor relationship. Her actions are not matching her request to be mentored. That may sound severe but your time is precious, and she should be putting some effort into the relationship as well.

If and when you do get a chance to meet with her, have a specific agenda. Address the issue head on but gently; be honest and kind. If she responds positively to you correction, express the need for goals. Make these goals measurable and give them a specific time frame; allow reasonable flexibility. Reassure her you will work with her on these goals, but you are also going to hold her accountable.

This is not a time to tear her down but to teach an encourage change. Pour out grace on her and let her know she is loved. Check in with her in non-judgmental ways. Be specific about when and how you will check in with her, like a text or a phone call. Do so privately—don't discuss it in front of others unless she initiates the conversation.

Before you part from your goal-setting conversation, give her one or two things to work on. More than that will be overwhelming to her. Reassure her again you are here to help her and encourage her, not to beat her over the head with a Bible or shame her. You're in it for the long haul.

If she truly wants to grow in Christ and your motivation is to help her, you will see change. She will make mistakes—give her grace. She is trying to break a life habit. At a minimum it will take 21 days. Recognize this is a process and will not be a quick fix. Any change will truly encourage you to continue with the relationship.

As the relationship deepens, more intimate situations will be shared. Your conversations may run the gamut of faith, family, career, love, marriage, and ministry. These important life direction topics inspire each of us to move forward; concentrate on the next step. The purpose in these discussions is to bring God's big picture for their life into clearer focus.

That may sound intimidating, but it is not as intense as it may appear. Remember you can always voice your own uncertainty. Even the apostle Paul saw God's plan dimly. "Now we see things imperfectly, like puzzling reflections in a mirror, but then we will see everything with perfect clarity. All that I know now is partial and incomplete, but then I will know everything completely, just as God now knows me completely" (I Corinthians 13:12 NLT). You don't need all the answers, you just need to be present.

Your words carry weight because of the investment you make. They listen due to the kindness we share. When you do speak, speak life. Even if you need to correct, do it in a way that encourages growth.

Proverbs 18:20-21 reminds us to share wisdom. "Wise words satisfy like a good meal; the right words bring satisfaction. The tongue can bring death or life; those who love to talk will reap the consequences." Stop right there—yes you do have wisdom to share. Faith in Jesus, reverence for Him, births wisdom in each of us (See Proverbs 9:10). Jesus directs your paths and gives you the right words to say.

On the other end of the spectrum, WARNING—do not become the mouth piece of God for them. This is way too much responsibility for you and you will fail. If this becomes your role you become a god-figure to them. This is dangerous for both of you. Your job is to direct them toward Jesus and away from dependence on you.

The Worthwhile Investment

> What a delight that God would find a way to care for me when I am caring for others.

Like with any investment there is a payoff. With some young friends it is large, while with some it can appear as a loss. With time, you may see the initial loss grow into a large dividend. Overall, I have learned it is worth it. I've seen growth, not only in them but in me as well! I didn't expect that. What a delight that God would find a way to care for me when I am caring for others. You've heard it over and over but it's true—you cannot out give Jesus.

Jesus taught this principle in the parable of the ten servants. (See Luke 19:11-27.) Oh how I want to hear "well done" when I see Him face to face! I'm sure you do, too. You have something to invest.

Time, income, and skills are all at your disposal to share with others. In Luke 19:26 Jesus shares his heart on investing: "'Yes,' the king replied, 'and to those who use well what they are given, even more will be given. But from those who do nothing, even what little they have will be taken away." You invest not just for the gain but because you love Jesus.

This is how many are introduced to a personal relationship with Jesus. A parent, Sunday school teacher, friend, church leader, or someone completely different...all of them are just ordinary people like you and me. Simply to love as Jesus loved. That certainly sounds like a worthwhile investment to me!

Of course, rejection is the number one fear. It is a real possibility. Remember, however, rejection does not measure your worth. Your worth is anchored in Jesus and Jesus alone. You were worth dying for. End of story. Jesus was rejected and He extended love anyway.

Follow His example: Jesus initiated the relationship with others. He invited his disciples to follow him. (Matthew 9:9) He set the example. He initiated with an invitation but left it to the followers to choose. It is a fine balance. You want them to know you are interested but you don't want to harass them into something. You want them to invest in the commitment.

Thousands of years ago, the biblical writers instructed each generation to teach the next. The instruction is found in Deuteronomy, the Psalms, and the epistles. The truth stays the same, but the method is adapted for the generation. We stand on the Word of God, instructing from it with grace. Paul beautifully expressed this to the Colossians: "This same Good News that came to you is going out all over the world. It is bearing fruit everywhere by changing lives, just as it changed your lives from the day you first heard and understood the truth about God's wonderful grace" (Colossians 1:6 NLT).

The Fruit of the Spirit

Obviously, you don't continually just quote Scripture while you are together. You do however, live your life based on the truth of the Gospel. Jesus is at the center of all your relationships. When others look at you they should see Him, not you. The fruits of His Spirit (Galatians 5:22-23) are to be part of who you are, not because you

> The Holy Spirit is saying "Stop hiding child. Share my fruit with others."

strive to produce them but because you spend time with Jesus, and they just kind of come out. The more intimate you are with Jesus the more you reflect Him. Your ability to share love, kindness, joy, patience, goodness, peace, gentleness, faithfulness, and self-control with your young friend is amplified as you give Jesus a chance to grow these fruits in you. And eventually, your display of fruit rubs off, and your young friend's fruit gets a booster shot. Kindness breeds kindness; joy is contagious; peace multiplies; patience, goodness, faithfulness, self control—they all have a snowball effect. Even in a hard-hearted person, child-like joy can be found and grown.

The Holy Spirit is saying "Stop hiding child. Share my fruit with others."

It's easy to get caught up in your own agenda. Self-focused and determined to check off your to-do list, you miss opportunities to share Jesus and His fruit. Let's be honest—the world needs more kindness, love, joy, and peace. And those things are contagious. When you're out the next time, make eye contact with the people you meet in passing. They might even smile back when you smile at them. It's contagious. That's the fruit of the

Spirit at work!

This is a simple truth but so often we forget about it and don't live it. But now is the time to be difference makers. It is time to stand out, be unique. Share your smile. Give a pleasant greeting; it may be the only kindness that individual receives. We live in a harsh world, and I want others to see me and ask "Why is she so nice?" The answer? Jesus.

"Instead, be kind to each other, tenderhearted, forgiving one another, just as God through Christ has forgiven you" (Ephesians 4:32 NLT).The word kind, in Greek (the original language of the New Testament) is chrestos. It also means "useful for others." Isn't that beautiful? Who knew such a small action could in and of itself a service to others. When you are kind you become a safe place for others in a hostile world. That is always my goal with the young women I talk with—kindness, and ultimately, service.

Wuv, Twu Wuv

One of the most difficult struggles to watch is their search for love. We are hard wired for relationship. I look back at my own life and I see God's hand as I was directed to my husband, Dave. My two oldest sisters were married right out of college, and here I was half-way through my twenties and alone. I hated it. I feared I would be alone for life.

That fear is as real today as it was for me. And the greater that desire in them, the more "desperate" they can appear. Wise words are necessary; remind your young pining women that a husband will not complete them. A spouse is meant to enhance life, not replace it. Your goal is to remind them of who they are in Christ. Direct them to find inner confidence based on Jesus, not life's circumstances. It is delicate balance, but an oh so important conversation.

Make sure they know you value you them no matter their marital status. Unfortunately many comments are made whether directed toward them or not that communicate they are not enough if they're single. Affirm their point in life. Don't just be interested in their love life, but their entire love. Make sure they know you value them and consider them to be whole without a spouse. Watch your words; be sure you aren't sending messages you don't mean to be sending about their worth.

To speak life means to speak love—love that draws out the image of God inside of them. It does help to chisel away circumstantial excess created by the messiness of life. It may be painful, but it's the good kind of pain—like after a day of exercise, where your muscles are sore because they were used in the way they were intended. We're instructed to stretch and challenge each another, but always in a way that brings health and wellness to our soul, not damage. Affirm the pain they're feeling is good and not injurious.

Part of the Deal: Dreams, Mistakes, Failures, and Success

This generation of dreamers needs to know they can achieve their God-directed goals. Of course, cheer them on and find words to console them in failure—for it is part of pursuing life and teaches as much as success does. Encourage them to take steps of faith. Not just a step but a faith-filled Jesus-is-gonna-catch-me jump! He will guide their path but He won't make them go, and neither can you. They need to initiate and trust God to do the rest.

Mistakes will happen—I mean yours, not just theirs. Trust me, my foot has been firmly planted in my mouth more than once. It is not appetizing nor will yours be. But when this happens (because it will), own it. Be authentic. Apologize and take time to learn from the mistake, but don't dwell on it. Move on. "Forgetting the past and looking forward to what lies ahead, I press on…" (Philippians 3:13-14 NLT).

The Investment—It's Worth It

What growth have I seen? I thought you'd never ask!

-A young woman overcome potentially debilitating health issues and financial struggles. Last December she will graduate from nursing school.

-Another struggled with her confidence. She has since traveled to Africa three times. She gained leadership skills which she is already using and, not to mention, she is now mentoring others.

-Another is now serving on staff at a local church.

All have gained confidence, leaning into the Lord to see what He is calling them to be. What joy to walk in this journey with them!

There is my directive—Christ, Coffee, and Caring. Nothing to do with coffee, really, unless you're me. Everything to do about Christ and caring.

Your turn. Pray about God's call for you in mentoring. Christ first—He is to be at the center of each of these relationships. What vehicle will you use? Coffee? Tea? Ice Cream? Walking? Running? Find your sweet spot and go with it. Finally, caring—your goal is to communicate that they matter. They are important to God and to you.

Dear Lord: Help us to have ears to hear the younger church. Help us to guide and love them as they are. Show us how you want us to meet together so we each feel comfortable. We ask for your wisdom. In Jesus Name AMEN.

Questions:

1. What must we "wear" when we mentor?

2. What vehicle will you use to meet with younger people? What neutral place or activity would make everyone comfortable?

3. Why do we look at ourselves first before we correct others? Do you need to ask yourself anything else before you give corrections?

4 How can we show others we care? What ways are comfortable for you?

Chapter Thirteen—The Reward

One of my favorite Shakespeare quotes is from A Midsummer Night's Dream. "And though she be but little she be fierce." As I am only 5'1" I like this quote a lot—not that I am an aggressive fighter...more like determined and intense in the pursuit of God's call. At least that's how I see

> You belong to God and you already have the victory.

it. But I know that I belong to God—and He has already won the victory (I John 4:4).

You, too, are fierce! You belong to God and you already have the victory. Don't forget that.

In this final chapter, I want to talk about the real reward of leaving a legacy.

Impact and Influence

Legacy is something handed down from one generation to the next. Legally it refers to money or property, but spiritual legacy does not just impact the here and now. You leave your fingerprints for eternity. Jesus gave us immortality, and we influence its impact the way we spend our finite time on earth.

Those are powerful words, "impact" and "influence." Impact implies a force. When your life intertwines with others, it is a force to be reckoned with! Your presence in their life isn't ignored; it may be quiet and gentle but it is steady. As a conduit of the Holy Spirit, you impact, while He shapes and changes them.

Influence is the capacity to have an effect on the character, development, or behavior of someone. What a beautiful way to describe mentoring! God uses you to bring out His design in another person; you are one of the tools used to expose their true beauty.

It reminds me of a young man I know who is a sculptor. He produces art from wood and stone. He examines the natural grain and sees an image. Through inspiration, time, and skill he produces a finished piece. Alec has a true gift.

Like Alec, you work similarly. Through God, you impact and influence to reveal God's image in another's life. Your tools range from encouragement to advice to accountability. You inspire, occasionally correct, and always love. You recognize God is the Ultimate Artist and you're simply an assistant. And you pray and pray and pray.

> You recognize God is the Ultimate Artist and you're simply an assistant.

As I write this, my daughter, Elizabeth, is attending an audition for a movie. Is it unlikely that she will be cast? Statistically, yes, but there is always a possibility. But her dream is to act; she won't get parts if she doesn't show up.

At the same time her younger sister is at a swim clinic. The instructors are Olympic swimmers. Will this make her a better swimmer? Yes. Will she now break records and get college scholarships? It could happen. We can't no the answer to that. But she, too, is in pursuit of a dream.

I'd like to think their inspiration comes from their dad and me. As parents, our children get first dibs on the legacy we are leaving behind. They are the epicenter of our impact within God's Kingdom. But our spiritual kids reap some of the ripple effect of that seismic wave. Later today, I'm going to a wedding shower for Jessica, who I meet with regularly. Together we share the joy of this life event!

At 52, this is the beginning of my legacy: lives that are encouraged and influenced to pursue something bigger than themselves.

Legacy Rewards

My friend Cheryl and her husband, Erik, mentor an entire group of young people. Their son organized a leadership/service group, which has opened the door for Cheryl and Erik to invite the whole group into their lives. Cheryl and Erik admit it can be overwhelming. They have felt inadequate more times than they like, and they have learned to walk the extra mile with no expectation of reward (Matthew 5:41).

But Cheryl talks about the genuine character of these college students. They are honest, even blunt, but she always knows where she stands with them. If she tries to break through a barrier to soon, they will become vague and pull away. They don't divulge any information until they feel safe, however paradoxical that may feel. It feels one-sided as they give but slowly they are seeing results.

Of course, rewards don't come free of frustration. During a service week, Cheryl had cooked dinner for them every night. On the last night, a young man came into the kitchen to remind her he didn't like what she was preparing. Can you feel her angst? After all this, now she has to make a special meal? But she went the extra mile, and in the end, the young man said he would try the original meal since she worked so hard. Yes, she was frustrated for sure. But then she realized the spiritual investment. She had patterned extra effort and going the extra mile for him, and he followed her example. Next time—hopefully—he would not need to ask for special treatment.

On the other hand, they're encouraged to see their students work hard for something bigger than themselves. Cheryl and Erik hosted students during a week long summer project. One young man wanted to participate but he could not take time off work, and his family needed the income. Each evening, he was dropped off for work at midnight and Erik picked him up at 4:30 AM so he could still participate. The young man lived on almost no sleep that week, all so he could be part of something bigger than himself. That is impactful. This is part of Cheryl and Erik's legacy, as well as the young man's.

The Reward of Trusting Jesus

One of the rewards I've gained throughout my ministry is greater trust in Jesus.

Jesus always shows up—not necessarily in the way we expect, but He always shows up. He guides us and guards us. As I have moved through this journey, my faith has increased. I continue in awe, as I see Him prove Himself over and over. With each new risk He calls me to, He honors my steps of faith. He redirects me when I take a misstep. He forgives when I mess up. It's a beautiful process.

He is faithful. Over the years I've survived countless awkward conversations. (You will too.) I have helped with jobs that required my sweat equity. Yes, that means I have actually contributed real sweat to get a job done—like garage sale set up and clean up on hot summer days and rescuing drivers in broken down cars. All for the sake of the relationship. My reward? Friendship.

And don't forget the phone calls. Many phone calls. Panicked phone calls. Teary phone calls. Angry phone calls. Sick phone calls. I've received them all. I have listened and listened and listened some more.

Oh, I'm not complaining—I've had tons of funny and joyful conversations, too! I've seen young adults work against the odds and achieve goals on the way to living their dreams. I've seen relationships bloom into engagements and marriages. What a beautiful gift to be part of their journey. And, joy of all joys in my heart—one young woman I've mentored is now mentoring other young women! I love every bit of it.

And my family has grown. In addition to my son and two biological daughters, I have many more spiritual daughters. It is a beautiful thing to love and be loved. Yes, there is heartache but there is so much more joy! Their successes produce a sense of satisfaction difficult to describe. It is

> "Children are a heritage from the Lord, offspring a reward from him."

beautiful and I want the same for you. I have a deeper understanding of Psalm 127—"Children are a heritage from the Lord, offspring a reward from him" (Psalm 127:3 NIV).

My community is stronger because it is multi-generational. I interact with individuals of all ages. I do this on purpose. For example, Elsie walked by me at an event last week. She is 72.

"How are you, daughter of my heart?" she said.

Hmm, I wonder why mentoring is important to me.

As I am finishing this process, I realized something funny about this book. My proofreader is 22. My editor is 26. My photographer is

23. I didn't do that on purpose but it was amusing when I recognized it. I am living this book through the process of writing it—I guess I needed proof of my own authenticity!

Final Rewards

I am convinced we cannot understand the full impact of our service on this side of Heaven. We do not do it for the reward. We do our part as it says in 1 Corinthians 3:8 (NIV)— "The one who plants and the one who waters have one purpose, and they will each be rewarded according to their own labor."

> Your legacy is a legacy of love and impact.

You are planting life in the soul of the next generation through the direction of the Holy Spirit. That in itself is a reward! Your legacy is a legacy of love and impact. One that says to another "You are worthy of my time. You are important. You can make an impact in this world for good."

So...are you in? Are you ready to enlarge your heart and welcome more young ones in? I guarantee they are waiting for you— you just have to say hello.

Go build your legacy

Dragonfly Ministry

Dragonfly Ministry was founded by Leslie Schonfeld in 2009. As a speaker and author, Leslie's goals are to help women to be confident, connected, and caring.

A dragonfly woman's confidence is centered on Jesus. She is connected in community in order to grow God's Kingdom. She cares for the next generation.

Why Dragonflies?

When my son was little we'd sit in our yard and watch the dragonflies. We loved counting them, guessing how many we might see. Some days, it would be dozens. It was our special time together. I still smile every time I see a dragonfly. Up close they are odd creatures. Yet, when they fly, their iridescent wings catch the light and they are dazzling. The same is true for us. Examine us closely and we all have imperfections, but when we fly in God's purpose, we too shimmer in the light of His glory.

Find out more about Dragonfly at www.dragonflyministry.com

Follow us on Facebook ,Twitter, and Instagram.

Leslie would love to speak at your next event. You can contact her at leslie@dragonflyministry.com

Notes

[1] Strongs Exhaustivo Bible Concordance Online." *Bible Study Tools*. Salem Web Network, 2014. Web. 26 Feb. 2016.